Insightful Parenting 1

Tailoring Your Parenting Style to Your Child's Temperament

Nathan K. Bryce, a dynamic educator and creator, has significantly impacted personal development and relationship dynamics. His extensive work includes books, training modules, blogs, videos, and online resources. His groundbreaking personality instrument, patented in 1994, has transformed global understanding of diverse temperaments. *Insightful Parenting* draws from this instrument, offering an in-depth look at parenting styles and child personality identification. Bryce emphasizes each temperament's strengths, equipping readers with tools to nurture positive traits and behaviors. His approach empowers individuals in various roles—parents, educators, mentors—promoting fulfilling relationships and deeper understanding of temperaments in family and professional spheres.

David Graff, a co-author of this book, exemplifies the roles of husband, father, grandfather, and friend. Married to Sara for over 41 years, they've raised seven children and welcomed 16 grandchildren. His experiences, deeply intertwined with the *Four Lenses* and his collaboration with Nathan Bryce, have profoundly shaped his life. In this volume, David shares the principles he's implemented to enhance his relationships and happiness. His journey, marked by both trials and successes, offers practical insights for family life. His work extends beyond personal life, significantly impacting military families worldwide with the *Four Lenses*. This book, a culmination of 25 years of wisdom, is David's hope for readers to build strong, resilient families.

Insightful Parenting 1

Tailoring Your Parenting Style to Your Child's Temperament

Published by Four Lenses | PO Box 138 | Riverton UT 84065-0089
+1 877 745 1566

©2023 Nathan K. Bryce, David B. Graff. All rights reserved.

No part of this book may be reproduced or transmitted in any form by any means—graphic, electronic, or mechanical, including photocopying, recording, or by any information storage and retrieval system—without permission in writing from the author and publisher, except when permitted by law.

The author and publisher disclaim all warranties with regard to the suitability of this book in predicting or changing behavior. In no event shall the author and publisher be liable for any indirect, incidental, special, or consequential damages out of or in connection with the furnishing, performance, or use of this book.

First printed: December 2023

10 9 8 7 6 5 4 3 2 1

Printed in the United States of America

ISBN 979-8-9882167-3-5

Acknowledgments

Reflecting on the essence of parenthood, my mind instinctively gravitates towards my own parents, Bob and Philis, undeniably among the finest examples of parental love and guidance. Their exceptional qualities are not just a son's biased view; the testimony comes from a larger circle of admiration—my seven elder siblings, their children, and even the succeeding generations. Each one echoes the sentiment of my parents' extraordinary nature. My earnest daily endeavor is to embody the values and lessons they have imparted.

Therefore, it is with deep gratitude and reverence that I dedicate this book to my wonderful parents. This work is not just a reflection of my thoughts on parenting but a tribute to their enduring legacy of love, sacrifice, and wisdom. They have always been my guiding stars, and it is in their honor that I share these insights, hoping to illuminate the path for others as they have illuminated mine.

—Nathan Bryce

Introduction

Rachel stood amidst the chaos of her living room, the evening air thick with tension. Her husband Ned's voice rose in frustration over the children's bickering, each word like a match igniting further discord. Emma, 14, retreated into her room, her face a canvas of hurt and confusion. Lucas, 9, sat rigidly, his homework forgotten, while Mia, 4, looked on bewildered, her innocent eyes reflecting the turmoil around her. Rachel felt a knot of helplessness tighten in her stomach. This wasn't the family life she had envisioned. The constant clashes, the misunderstandings, the emotional whirlwind—it all seemed to be spiraling out of control.

Ned, a man of routine and order, often found himself at odds with Rachel's more spontaneous nature. Their disagreements were frequent, with Ned's desire for structure clashing against Rachel's free-spirited approach. Emma, sensitive and introspective, often felt overwhelmed by the household's unrest. Lucas, who seemed to crave the same order as his father, was increasingly agitated by the unpredictable environment. And little Mia, with her boundless energy, often found herself caught in the crossfire of the family's conflicts.

The strain was evident. Rachel and Ned's relationship was fraying, each argument leaving a deeper scar. Rachel often lay awake at night, wondering how their once harmonious home had turned into a battleground of conflicting perspectives. She longed for a way to bridge the growing gaps, to bring back the laughter and understanding that once filled their home.

One evening, amid the remnants of yet another heated argument, Rachel found herself seeking solace in the quiet corner of a bookstore. Her eyes, weary and seeking answers, landed on a book titled *Insightful Parenting 1*. The back cover hinted at understanding parenting styles and children's temperaments—concepts Rachel had never considered but which sparked a flicker of hope in her. She purchased the book on the spot.

Back at home, as Rachel turned the pages, a new world unfolded before her. The book spoke of personality temperament, a concept foreign to her, but which resonated deeply. It described patterns of behavior, emotional responses, and ways of interacting with the world—insights that began to shed light on the turmoil in her family.

Insightful Parenting 1 introduced Rachel to the idea that each family member might be operating from a different temperamental base. It proposed that the clashes and misunderstandings were not just random occurrences but stemmed from fundamental personality differences in how they each experienced and responded to the world.

Rachel's mind raced with thoughts of Emma's quiet moments, Lucas's need for order, and Mia's curious explorations. She began to see Ned's insistence on routine and her own impulsive decisions in a new light. The book offered not just definitions but also real-life examples that mirrored her family's daily interactions.

The more Rachel read, the more she understood the root of their conflicts. The book suggested that recognizing and respecting each individual's unique personality could be the key to harmonizing their family life. It offered assessments to accurately measure her own parenting style, and the personality style of her children, regardless of their ages. It also promised strategies for communication, conflict resolution, and fostering emotional connections tailored to each temperament.

Armed with this new knowledge, Rachel felt a renewed sense of purpose. She saw a path to healing the rifts in her family, to nurturing her children's growth in a way that respected their individual needs, and to finding a middle ground with Ned. *Insightful Parenting 1* was more than a book; it was a lifeline, offering a chance to rebuild her family on a foundation of understanding and empathy.

As Rachel finished the book, she felt the first stirrings of optimism in a long time. The journey ahead would require patience, learning, and adaptation, but for the first time in a long while, Rachel felt equipped to face the challenges. She held the book close, a beacon of hope in her quest to restore peace and connection to her family.

Table of Contents

1 | Embracing Adaptive Parenting 1

2 | Parenting Style Assessment...25

3 | The Blue Parenting Style..35

4 | The Gold Parenting Style...53

5 | The Green Parenting Style..71

6 | The Orange Parenting Style..91

7 | How to Parent Aliens..109

8 | Observing the Behaviors of Children: Ages 0-3................129

9 | Observing the Behaviors of Children: Ages 4-7................155

10 | Measuring the Personality of Older Children 179

11 | Primary Color Quiz: Ages 8-9 189

12 | Primary Color Quiz: Ages 10-11 205

13 | Primary Color Quiz: Ages 12-13 221

14 | Primary Color Quiz: Ages 14-15 237

15 | Primary Color Quiz: Ages 16-17 257

16 | What's Next?...277

Chapter 1

Embracing Adaptive Parenting

Dive into the infinite gallery of parenting roles and experience the exhilaration and anxiety of the parenting rollercoaster. Learn how one-size-fits-all parenting styles don't always work and learn how to navigate the challenges, celebrate the joys, and oscillate through various parenting styles in this introductory chapter on adaptive parenting.

Embracing the Multifaceted Roles of Parenting

Ah, parenting! An exhilarating rollercoaster ride with intricate loops of joy, challenge, love, and at times, bafflement, anxiety, and a few blood-curdling screams.

While you're at this amusement part, imagine standing in the maze of mirrors, each reflecting a slightly different version of yourself—a kind guide, a strict guardian, a playful pal, or perhaps a wise mentor? As parents, every day we morph into myriad forms, seamlessly oscillating between various parenting roles, often without the conscious realization of doing so. Do any of these roles sound familiar?

> caregiver, teacher, protector, role model, friend, provider, mentor, playmate, disciplinarian, storyteller, chef, nurse, chauffeur, listener, counselor, cheerleader, coach, confidant, mediator, organizer, advocate, problem solver, advisor, motivator, entertainer, financial advisor, life skills instructor, guidance counselor, fashion consultant, personal shopper, event planner, homework helper, personal trainer, babysitter, guardian, travel companion, bedtime story reader, tech support, tutor, nurse, tooth fairy, conflict resolver, safety officer, career advisor, accountant, housekeeper, repairperson, lawn care specialist, pet caretaker, travel agent, photographer, personal assistant, hairstylist, barber, laundry expert, tech guru, alarm clock, nutritionist, driver's ed instructor, gardener, party planner, emergency responder, lifelong supporter

Each role, with its unique demands and rewards, intertwines with our intrinsic personality traits and temperaments and colors how we perform that role.

Welcome to the world of parenting styles, where we navigate through the vibrant personalities of Blue, Gold, Green, and Orange temperaments. Think of this book as your toolkit, where we'll discover how each temperament brings its own special spice to the parenting journey.

But that's not the only thing we'll discover, we'll also learn how to effectively identify the personalities of our children and how to parent them effectively. Ready to embark on this colorful adventure?

Imagine parenting as crafting a paper airplane. Each fold, each crease, is a conscious decision that shapes its flight path. Similarly, each parenting style—Blue, Gold, Green, and Orange—is a unique fold, shaping your child's personality and future trajectory.

The Essence of Parenting Styles

Venturing deeper into the vivid hues of our parenting styles, let's unearth the intrinsic essences that bedeck each color.

Meet the Blue parents—think of them as your friendly neighborhood therapists. Always there with a comforting word and a shoulder to lean on, they create a safe space where emotions flow freely.

Then we have the Gold parents—the planners, the organizers, the ones with a five-year plan. They build a structured world where rules are clear, and traditions are valued, ensuring a stable environment for their kids.

Enter the Green parents—the thinkers, the ponderers, the "why is the sky blue?" explorers. Their parenting style is a blend of logic and encouragement for curiosity, creating a space where questions are welcomed, and learning never stops.

And don't forget the Orange parents—the adventurers, the explorers, the "let's turn our living room into a pirate ship" kind of guides. Their world is one of spontaneity and fun, ensuring their children are always in for an exciting ride.

Each style, unique in its own right, combines to create a multifaceted approach to parenting.

In this book, we'll explore the four temperaments and parenting styles, learning how they complement and sometimes clash with each other, creating a melody of experiences and interactions.

Your temperament plays a pivotal role in shaping your parenting style. It influences your interactions, decisions, and even the challenges you might face in your parenting journey. For example, those with a reflective personality might find themselves naturally engaging in heartfelt conversations with their children, while those with an orderly personality might lean towards creating a structured family environment.

Our own personalities aren't the only players in this game. Ever found yourself mimicking your own parents, either replicating their methods or deliberately doing the opposite? It's fascinating how our parents' approaches sneak into our own, influencing our parenting style in subtle and not-so-subtle ways.

This exploration, recognizing the shadows of our parents within us, helps carve out a mindful path in our parenting journey. A path where understanding and acceptance guide us, allowing us to consciously choose our parenting narrative.

Additional Factors That Affect Our Parenting Practices

But wait, there's more! Let's explore some tangible examples that clearly demonstrate how external factors, such as social and cultural influences, also shape our parenting practices.

The "Successful" Child Narrative. Society often applauds children who excel academically, athletically, socially, or in other visible arenas, potentially pushing parents towards enforcing a rigorous, achievement-oriented environment, even if their natural style leans towards a more nurturing and liberal approach.

Gender Norms. Parents may inadvertently mold their boys to be strong and unemotional and their girls to be gentle and caring, adhering to socially normative stereotypes, regardless of the children's actual temperaments and preferences. This partially explains why many children and youth are confused and experience gender identity issues, associating masculinity and femininity to biological males or females, and why Blue males and Green females often struggle with their preferences, especially in their developmental years as they actively explore and brighten different aspects of their own personality spectrum.

Peer Pressure among Parents. Sometimes, seeing other parents enforce strict routines or enroll their children in numerous activities can make parents second-guess their own more laid-back, child-led parenting approach.

Educational Institutions' Philosophies. The underlying philosophy of the educational institutions that children attend—be it a focus on holistic development, academic rigor, or creative expression—can impact parenting approaches as parents might align their home environment and expectations to mirror educational values.

Emphasis on Grades. The educational system's focus on grades and standardized test scores might pressure even the most free-spirited, Orange parent to begrudgingly prioritize academics and structured study times at home.

Discipline Policies. If a school, sports team, or religious organization enforces strict disciplinary policies, parents may find themselves emphasizing similar stringent rules at home to maintain consistency for their child.

Homework Expectations. Parents might find themselves navigating a tightrope between being a facilitator and an enforcer as they try to balance the school's homework expectations with their child's need for play, solitary reflection, and relaxation.

Childhood Memories. A parent who experienced rigid discipline might either emulate this in their parenting style, believing in its effectiveness, or swing to the opposite spectrum, adopting a more permissive approach to spare their child similar experiences.

Work-life Balance. Parents who have experienced burnout in their professional life might prioritize downtime and leisure for their children, sometimes even if it contradicts societal expectations of enrolling children in various developmental activities.

Parenting Self-perception. If a parent has faced criticism or praise for their parenting style, these experiences might shape their future actions, either by sticking to their guns in defiance or altering their approach to gain approval.

Cultural Expectations. The cultural context in which parents are raising their children often dictates specific norms and values, guiding parenting behaviors and expectations even if they might not align with a parent's instinctual style. For instance, collectivist cultures might encourage more authoritarian parenting, emphasizing respect and obedience, while individualist cultures might lean towards promoting autonomy and self-expression in children.

Technological Advances. The pervasive role of technology and social media can influence parenting styles by introducing varied perspectives on upbringing, potentially causing parents to question or modify their own approaches. Parents might find themselves swaying between embracing digital literacy and enforcing screen-time restrictions to foster balanced development in their children.

Parenting Books and Expert Advice. Exposure to various parenting books, blogs, and expert advice could either affirm or challenge existing parenting styles, prompting parents to either bolster their current approaches or pivot towards new strategies to align with perceived best practices.

Financial Stability. Economic conditions and financial stability can significantly sway parenting styles. Parents who are financially stable might have the bandwidth to explore varied activities and resources for their children, while those facing economic challenges might prioritize basic needs, potentially influencing their approach towards discipline, academics, and recreational activities.

Community and Neighborhood Environment. The community and environment in which a family resides often dictate acceptable norms and behaviors. A neighborhood that values community involvement and social interactions might influence parents to adopt a more socially oriented and permissive parenting style, while those in highly competitive environments might enforce more structured and achievement-oriented approaches.

Global Influences and Events. Global events such as pandemics, natural disasters, war, or political upheavals might shift parenting priorities and approaches, emphasizing values like resilience, empathy, or activism, and potentially altering day-to-day parenting practices and long-term aspirations for children.

Personal Beliefs and Values. Parental values and beliefs, shaped by personal experiences, religious beliefs, and philosophical alignments, play a pivotal role in crafting parenting styles, and can be subject to alteration when exposed to contrasting worldviews or life-altering experiences.

Child's Health and Abilities. A child's health condition or special abilities might necessitate alterations in parenting styles to accommodate, nurture, and advocate for their unique needs, sometimes requiring a blend of varied approaches to ensure holistic development and wellbeing. In fact, certain mental, physical, and emotional conditions can entirely mask the innate personality preferences of your children, especially if they are unable to achieve the things they intrinsically value and find themselves in a perpetual state of low self-worth or despair.

In each of these scenarios, the parent's intrinsic parenting style is nudged, negotiated, or sometimes hijacked by external influences, urging a constant reevaluation and adaptation of their parenting strategies in real-time. The underlying theme here resonates with the continual dance between staying true to one's parenting convictions while also navigating the multifaceted pressures and expectations of the external environment. Isn't it a riveting, albeit challenging, navigation through the vast seas of parenting?

Whether it is societal whispers encouraging the empathetic Blue to perhaps harden, or the educational norms urging the structured Gold to flex, our parenting styles, while deeply rooted, are often swayed or fortified by the external and experiential winds that breeze through our journey. Intriguingly, these winds sometimes introduce us to new horizons, allowing us to explore uncharted territories in our parenting adventure.

The Impact of Our Dominant Parenting Style

In the intricate tapestry of parenting, our threads of practices and beliefs weave a pattern that is often emblematic of our predominant parenting style. Picture a Blue parent, bestowing a cascade of emotional support upon their child, anchoring their actions in empathy and connection. Contrast this with the Green parent, where rationality and strategic encouragement carve out a path for a child's development. Now, imagine these intrinsic defaults activating the moment your child navigates through challenges and triumphs. Our default mode not only colors our everyday interactions but also silently communicates values and beliefs to our little ones, doesn't it?

Reflect upon the following original poem, which draws its inspiration from the insightful piece penned in 1954 by Dorothy Law Nolte, aptly titled "Children Learn What They Live." Within the stanzas of our new poem, we navigate through some of the admirable virtues attributed to each of the four temperaments, inviting a contemplative pause: wouldn't we desire our children to embody all of these enriching qualities rather than the handful that are associated with our own primary color?

How Our Conduct Molds Our Children

If children live with acceptance, they learn love.
If children live with empathy, they learn compassion.
If children live with boundaries, they learn respect.
If children live with laughter, they learn joyfulness.
If children live with exploration, they learn curiosity.
If children live with support, they learn confidence.
If children live with integrity, they learn honesty.
If children live with celebration, they learn gratitude.
If children live with discipline, they learn structure.
If children live with understanding, they learn patience.
If children live with justice, they learn fairness.
If children live with encouragement, they learn ambition.
If children live with companionship, they learn friendship.
If children live with creativity, they learn innovation.
If children live with stability, they learn security.
If children live with mindfulness, they learn presence.
If children live with freedom, they learn self-expression.
If children live with gentleness, they learn tenderness.
If children live with humility, they learn selflessness.
If children live with tolerance, they learn harmony.

> If children live with persistence, they learn determination.
> If children live with orderliness, they learn organization.
> If children live with prudence, they learn caution.
> If children live with autonomy, they learn self-determination.
> If children live with optimism, they learn hopefulness.
> If children live with playfulness, they learn light-heartedness.

Does our instinctive parenting style align more closely with our personal needs, or with those inherent to our child's temperament? This ostensibly simple question reveals a myriad of introspective layers and invites potential recalibrations in our parenting journey, forging a path towards more flexibility, deeper relationships, and synergistic development.

After we thoroughly review the four primary parenting styles described in this book, we will then delve deeper into the realms of our children's personalities, and you'll find assessments and advice to help you during this discovery process.

Perhaps you'll find that an enlightening, albeit sometimes perplexing disparity surfaces, mirroring the diverse needs and inherent styles of our offspring. A Gold parent, firm in structure and routine, may unknowingly stifle the vibrant, impulsive spirit of an Orange child, whose world blossoms in spontaneity and adventure. And oh, the dance of adaptation we embark upon in these moments! How do we marry the systematic, orderly world of a Gold parent with the ever-changing, dynamic canvas upon which an Orange child paints their experiences?

This disparity, rich in learning and opportunities, beckons parents to don a hat of flexibility, fostering an environment where the child feels seen, heard, and fundamentally, understood. It's a high wire balancing act, isn't it? Nurturing their essence while also imparting the wisdom and boundaries that parenting undeniably calls for.

Now consider this: a Green parent, whose world orbits around logic and analytical thinking, encounters their Blue child's emotional meltdown. The parent, leaning into their dominant style, may offer logical solutions, inadvertently overlooking the emotional validation the child seeks. The child, awash with feelings, finds themselves adrift in a sea of misunderstood emotions, while the parent is anchored to the shores of reason and analysis, both seemingly lost in translation.

In another vignette, a Gold parent, valuing discipline and structure, may find themselves at odds with their Green teenager who challenges rules with logical arguments and seeks autonomy in decision-making. The ensuing tug of war could morph into a chasm of misunderstanding, couldn't it? Exploring these misalignments lays bare the delicate threads that weave the parent-child relationship, illuminating pathways towards enhanced communication, empathy, and mutual respect.

Visualize a scenario where a child struggles with academic pressures. A Blue parent might envelope the child in a cocoon of emotional support, creating a safe haven for expression. On the other end of the spectrum, a Gold parent might implement structured study plans and seek external help to navigate through the academic maze. Contrastingly, a Green parent may dissect the problem analytically, strategizing solutions, while an Orange parent might encourage breaks, infusing moments of lightness and leisure to counterbalance stress.

Each lens, unique and valid in its own right, provides divergent pathways through the same challenge. The converging point remains: understanding and respect for diverse parenting styles, intertwining them with the child's inherent nature, carving a path that fosters growth, well-being, and harmonious parent-child relationships.

The Multifaceted Parent: Adapting to Our Partner and Children

If there are two parents in our homes, we intertwine both parenting philosophies, each dyed with the unique shades of our temperaments. Imagine a Blue parent, the empathetic, always-there-with-a-hug kind, teaming up with a Green parent, the logical, "let's solve this puzzle" type. It's like having a heart and a brain working together to navigate the rollercoaster of raising a kid. The Blue parent showers emotional support, while the Green parent fuels intellectual growth. When understood and valued, their combined efforts can create a harmonious and well-rounded guide for a child through life's many paths.

But what happens when these styles clash? The Blue might see the Green as distant, while the Green might think the Blue is a bit too mushy. Understanding and appreciating these differences can illuminate their beauty, showcasing how they can collaboratively offer a child a balanced upbringing, ensuring both emotional and intellectual growth.

Now, let's talk about the genuine superheroes: single parents who navigate the parenting maze without a co-pilot. Single parents juggle various parenting styles, blending them without the collaborative input a partner might provide. They are the provider, the guide, and the emotional anchor, all rolled into one, adapting their style to meet their child's ever-changing needs. How does a single, steadfast parent incorporate playful, spontaneous, or nurturing elements into their parenting while journeying solo through parenthood? It's a challenging yet beautiful opportunity to craft a colorful, multi-dimensional parenting approach, fostering an environment where parent and child grow, learn, and adapt together.

Insightful Parenting 1 ■ 13

Whether parenting solo or with a partner, looking through the colorful lens into our children's world, we see a spectrum of needs and desires. Imagine a household where a free-spirited Orange child and a detail-oriented Gold sibling coexist. The Orange dances in the moment, while the Gold finds solace in structured routines. How do we weave a net that envelops them both, catering to their divergent needs while providing understanding and validation?

In this rich diversity, there's a garden of opportunities and potential struggles, where empathy and respect must be carefully nurtured. It's a dance of ensuring one child's need for routine doesn't overshadow another's desire for spontaneity, and vice versa. A balance must be struck, nurturing their individualities while also cultivating a family environment that thrives amidst these varied needs, validating and respecting each individual, wouldn't you agree?

Harmony within the family emerges through understanding, adaptation, and compromise. Imagine a family where each member embodies a different temperament. A Green parent might naturally nurture the curiosity of a Green child, while perhaps finding it challenging to navigate the emotional world of a Blue child. How do we ensure the family environment doesn't favor a particular temperament, neglecting the inherent needs of the others?

Wonderful relationships are forged through mutual respect, open communication, and a commitment to fostering an environment where each temperament is celebrated and understood. It demands a conscious effort to ensure each parenting style and child's temperament is acknowledged and validated, enabling the family to navigate life's journey in a way that respects and uplifts each individual. In this enriched environment, every member blossoms, learning from the varied hues of one another, shaping a vibrant, multifaceted family life.

Moreover, instilling the value of reciprocal appreciation and accommodation towards others' preferences is pivotal in this colorful family journey. It's vital that children not only receive understanding and acknowledgment of their own temperamental colors but also learn from and appreciate the distinct hues of their family members' personalities. By parents exemplifying flexibility and adaptability in their interactions, children are more likely to mature into individuals who can graciously bend and willingly forfeit their own desires at times, all in the service of expressing love and consideration towards their loved ones, thereby weaving a stronger, more harmonious family tapestry.

Enumerating the Benefits of Adaptive Parenting

In the delicate dance of parenting, one of the most melodic tunes that can resonate within the walls of a household is that of fortified, resilient relationships between parent and child. Imagine, the parent adapting, pivoting, and molding their style in tune with the unique, emerging personality of their child. It's like being a shapeshifter, but instead of turning into a wolf or a bird, you're navigating through the various shades of parenting. There's something truly enchanting about a child feeling seen, heard, and loved in their own unique, quirky ways, isn't there?

Building a relationship with your child isn't just about understanding them but also about building a sturdy bridge of trust and open communication. Consider a Green parent, a logical thinker, trying to decipher the colorful, emotion-laden world of an Orange child. It's like a scientist trying to understand an artist. But oh, the beautiful tapestry they weave when they step into each other's worlds, creating connections that are both profound and resilient, weathering the storms of time and challenge.

And what about us, the parents, as we mirror our child's needs and emotional worlds? Do we not also embark on a journey into our own emotional and psychological landscapes, discovering new facets of our personality? A structured, meticulous Gold parent might just find themselves on a rollercoaster of spontaneity and flexibility, trying to connect with their vibrant Orange child, exploring uncharted territories of their own personality.

This exchange becomes a lush field where both parent and child grow, mutually influencing each other's development. As parents weave through the various styles, children, too, soak up these experiences, learning empathy, adaptability, and understanding, planting seeds for their own evolution.

Imagine a family where adaptive parenting is the gentle wind, nurturing every member. A Gold parent, traditionally appreciative of order, intertwining their style with the dynamic needs of a Green child, creates an atmosphere where every individual is a cherished note in a beautiful symphony. Can such an atmosphere, where every individual feels valued and respected, not foster a familial environment bubbling with positivity and mutual respect?

This environment becomes a sanctuary where every member, despite their varied temperaments, coexists harmoniously, understanding and adapting to each other's worlds. The subtle acknowledgment of each other's intrinsic nature and a conscious effort to comprehend and cater to them weave a family tapestry that is resilient, vibrant, and deeply interconnected, enhancing the emotional climate of the household.

In the grand theatre of social interactions, children, adorned with the experiences of adaptive parenting, become adept at navigating through myriad social scenarios with grace and empathy. A child, having witnessed and been the recipient of adaptive, flexible parenting, naturally imbibes these qualities in their own social interactions, enabling them to build robust, empathetic connections with diverse individuals.

This capability not only enhances their social experiences but also becomes a foundation upon which they build their relationships outside the familial domain. Engaging with peers, educators, and eventually colleagues, they carry forward the legacy of adaptability, understanding, and emotional intelligence, contributing to the creation of empathetic, understanding environments wherever they go.

Emotional intelligence, a treasure in the realm of interpersonal relationships, is often cultivated within the crucible of adaptive parenting. A child, nestled within an environment that mirrors emotional understanding and adaptability, naturally develops a rich emotional vocabulary and understanding. A Blue parent, sailing through the emotional seas of their Gold child, fosters not only a secure attachment but also imparts the tacit knowledge of emotional navigation and understanding.

Moreover, resilience, a robust tree that shelters from life's tempests, finds its seeds in the understanding, validation, and adaptive nurturance provided by the parent. The child learns that their emotional world is not only understood and respected but also that it is safe to explore, express, and navigate through it. This sense of security and emotional validation lays a strong foundation, upon which the child builds their edifice of emotional intelligence and resilience, navigating through life's varied landscapes with an intrinsic understanding and empathy towards themselves and others.

Significance of Delving Deeper into Each Parenting Style

Embarking on a journey through the intricacies of various parenting styles opens a new realm of understanding and connection within the familial context. As parents, guardians, or anyone who plays a pivotal role in shaping a child's development, diving deep into understanding distinct parenting styles transcends the surface-level knowledge, immersing into the profound seas of empathetic, responsive, and effective parenting. This will be the primary subject of the next few chapters. We will attempt to measure your own parenting preferences, and then, we will spend a chapter on each of the four cardinal parenting styles.

After assessing and exploring the various parenting styles, we will then turn our focus over to the children. We'll first look at several age-appropriate assessments that your children can complete, and then we'll spend chapter after chapter exploring how children of each temperament prefer to interact in specific, real-life settings.

By exploring each style—Blue, Gold, Green, and Orange— with curiosity and open-mindedness, we gain more than just knowledge; we unlock a treasure trove of empathetic connections, whereby we can resonate with our children's emotional and social landscapes, navigating through their joys, challenges, dreams, and fears with nuanced sensitivity and support.

Furthermore, understanding each personality style is akin to acquiring a valuable toolkit, empowering us with the means to mend gaps, build bridges, and forge stronger, more authentic relationships with our children. As we unveil the characteristics, strengths, and challenges embedded in each style, we learn the art of aligning our parenting approaches with our children's intrinsic needs, crafting an environment where they feel seen, heard, and deeply understood. In this rich soil of understanding and emotional nourishment, we foster not just the growth of our children, but also the blossoming of a harmonious family life, wherein every member feels valued and cherished for their authentic selves.

Igniting the flame of curiosity as we advance further into our expedition of parenting and personality styles is quintessential. To immerse ourselves in this journey is not merely to absorb information, but to weave this newfound knowledge into the very fabric of our familial interactions and relationships. The path ahead, while enlightening, also beckons us to embody a spirit of flexibility and adaptability, as we learn to mold our parenting approaches in resonance with our children's evolving needs, personalities, and aspirations.

Embarking on a Parenting Adventure Together

Welcome to the start of a new chapter of your life, where an exciting exploration of parenting styles is about to unfold! We're not just here to share insights that could lift your parenting to new heights, but to help you and your loved ones find more happiness and success in life. So, this isn't just a call to read hundreds of pages, but an invitation to dive in, reflect, and actively mingle with the insights ahead, allowing them to dance with your parenting instincts and deepen your connections with your children.

Engaging with the chapters ahead is a gift to your children and to yourself. It's a pledge to evolve, to step forward with an open heart and mind, ready to adapt and grow alongside your little ones. As we delve into each parenting style, wrapping our understanding around their subtleties, we're crafting a story that braids informed, adaptive parenting with the lively, dynamic worlds of our children.

To help you reflect and incorporate what you are reading into your life, here are some engaging questions and prompts to ponder upon as you read through the rest of the content in this book.

1. Which aspects of the discussed parenting styles resonated most with you and why?
2. Were there moments within the chapter that gently nudged against your established beliefs?
3. Can you recall instances where a clash of parenting styles became evident in your family?
4. How do you perceive the impact of your dominant parenting style on your child's development?
5. Can you identify instances where adopting a different parenting style might have altered an outcome?
6. How has your own parents' style influenced your approach towards parenting?
7. In what ways do you believe understanding different parenting styles will benefit your family?
8. Are there fears or resistances that surface at the thought of altering your parenting style?
9. How do you feel your parenting style aligns or clashes with that of your partner?
10. Can you recall a moment where understanding your child's personality type could have shifted an interaction?
11. How can you employ strategies from different parenting styles to communicate with your child more effectively?

12. In what areas do you believe your current parenting style may be falling short and how can you address this?
13. What steps can you take to ensure that your parenting approach fosters a healthy emotional environment for your child?
14. How can you create a balance between asserting authority and allowing autonomy in your parenting?
15. How do your own emotional needs and personality traits influence your parenting decisions and style?
16. Can you identify the aspects of your child's temperament that might be in opposition to your natural parenting inclinations?
17. How might you navigate discussions with your partner about potentially conflicting parenting styles or philosophies?
18. How will you navigate the challenge of maintaining consistency in your parenting approach, especially during stressful times?
19. What strategies can you employ to remain adaptable and flexible in your parenting, even when faced with unexpected challenges?
20. How might you better support and encourage the innate temperamental traits of your child, even if they diverge from your own?
21. How do you plan to address and manage any potential bias towards your own temperament when interacting with your child?
22. In what ways can you ensure that your parenting does not stifle your child's natural propensities and traits?
23. How will you ensure that your child feels heard and validated, even when their perspective diverges from your own?

24. How can you teach your child to respect and appreciate temperamental differences in their peers and other individuals?

25. Are there instances where you might need to seek support or further resources to aid your adaptive parenting journey?

These questions are designed to gently guide your reflections, inviting you to dive deeper into your own experiences, perceptions, and anticipations regarding the parenting styles explored within this chapter. Pondering upon them not only deepens your engagement with the content but also prepares your heart and mind to embrace the depth and diversity that the upcoming chapters promise to unfold. Let them stir within your heart and mind thoughtful contemplation, providing a fertile ground where the seeds of insights from the upcoming chapters can take root and flourish.

25 Reasons to Adopt Adaptive Parenting

To help you decide if you want to continue reading or not, here are 25 benefits that showcase various angles and facets of the impact of adaptive parenting on both the immediate family environment and the wider society, attempting to touch upon different aspects such as emotional intelligence, interpersonal relationships, societal harmony, and personal and societal well-being.

1. Adaptive parenting equips children with robust conflict-resolution skills, enabling them to navigate disagreements in a healthy and constructive manner.

2. It enables children to seamlessly integrate into various social contexts by understanding and adapting to diverse personality dynamics.

3. The approach of understanding and valuing all personality styles teaches children the invaluable skill of tolerance in multifaceted societal interactions, tolerance that rises above skin color, ethnicity, nationality, socio-economic status, sexual preference, political party, religious affiliation, and every other "us vs. them" tribal identity.

4. Children become adept at recognizing and appreciating the strengths inherent in different personality styles, fostering environments of mutual respect and admiration.

5. Such parenting facilitates an inclusive approach towards varied learning and interaction styles, promoting educational environments that cater to diverse strengths and needs.

6. Children, when exposed to adaptive parenting, are more likely to contribute to creating supportive peer environments, thereby reducing instances of bullying and isolation.

7. The practice of adaptive parenting promotes mental health wellness by providing emotional validation and support tailored to each child's unique personality.

8. Children develop a balanced perspective, valuing their own personality style while simultaneously appreciating the differences inherent in others.

9. An adaptive parent inherently fosters a home environment where the unique emotional and social needs of each child are acknowledged and catered to.

10. Such parenting propels children towards developing friendships that are emotionally rich and socially supportive, enhancing their social lives.

11. The comprehensive understanding of different personality styles enables children to become effective team players in varied group dynamics.

12. Children learn the art of constructive feedback, understanding how to communicate critiques in a manner that respects varied personality sensitivities.
13. Adaptive parenting naturally fosters environments where emotional expression is valued and encouraged, enhancing emotional communication within the family.
14. It contributes towards the development of vibrant communities, where each individual's unique contributions are valued and celebrated.
15. Children nurtured in adaptive environments become adept at leveraging the strengths of varied personalities in collaborative endeavors.
16. They learn to navigate through the challenges posed by personality clashes with understanding and adaptability.
17. Adaptive parenting provides children with a safe space where they can explore and understand their own evolving personality style without judgment or rigid expectations.
18. It significantly reduces the potential for generational conflicts by fostering an understanding of varied personality and interaction styles across different age demographics.
19. Adaptive parenting nurtures emotionally secure adults, who then contribute towards creating workplaces that are supportive and understanding.
20. It fosters the development of leaders who are adept at managing and leading teams composed of varied personality styles effectively.
21. Children are better prepared to navigate through the varied personality dynamics present in different cultural contexts, enhancing their adaptability in a globalized world.

22. The understanding of varied personality styles enhances a child's ability to engage in empathetic customer service, understanding and catering to diverse client needs.

23. Children are able to make informed career choices that are in alignment with their personality style, enhancing professional satisfaction and success.

24. Adaptive parenting contributes towards breaking the cycle of rigid, normative parenting, paving the way for generations of emotionally rich parenting practices.

25. The nurturing of emotional adaptability in children enhances their capability to manage the varied emotional and social dynamics present in intimate relationships, contributing towards the development of healthy and long-lived partnerships.

"If you want to change the world, go home and love your family."

—Mother Teresa

Chapter 2

Parenting Style Assessment

Identify your dominant parenting style with the 20-item Parenting Style Assessment. This survey will measure the way you currently prefer to parent. The results may or may not correlate with your personality as measured by other instruments.

Instructions

You are about to take a simple 20-question parenting style assessment. It measures how each parenting style responds to ten different categories: emotional support, guidance and discipline, fostering independence, encourage healthy lifestyle, social skills and relationships, intellectual and cognitive development, confidence and self-esteem, ethical and moral development, encouraging creativity and self-expression, and problem solving and coping skills.

As you read each question, select the one answer that most accurately represents you in your current state, not based on how you aspire to be or how others perceive you should parent. Consider your present tendencies and preferences, rather than idealized versions of yourself. Even if you do not have children or grandchildren in your home, envision how you would prefer to respond if you did.

Assessment

1. As a parent, I give my children:
    - _____ A. Security, dependability, and direction.
    - _____ B. Energy, excitement, and adventure.
    - _____ C. Affection, compassion, and communication.
    - _____ D. Knowledge, reason, and expertise.

2. With my children, I prefer to play the role of:
    - _____ E. Consultant, Analyst, Observer.
    - _____ F. Caretaker, Guardian, Manager.
    - _____ G. Ringleader, Cohort, Trainer.
    - _____ H. Nurturer, Therapist, Supporter.

Insightful Parenting 1 ■ 27

3. I want my children to be:
    _____ A. Obedient, careful, accountable, ambitious, disciplined.
    _____ B. Lively, noticed, satisfied, animated, victorious.
    _____ C. Happy, accepted, tolerant, kindhearted, comfortable.
    _____ D. Inquisitive, self-directed, broad-minded, capable.

4. When leaving for the day, I encourage my children to:
    _____ E. "Think it through".
    _____ F. "Do the right thing".
    _____ G. "Go for it".
    _____ H. "Follow your heart".

5. I prefer my children to be:
    _____ A. Responsible, dependable, morally straight.
    _____ B. Dynamic, talented, physically strong.
    _____ C. Genuine, distinctive, emotionally stable.
    _____ D. Clever, resourceful, mentally awake.

6. It is important that my children are able to successfully:
    _____ E. Develop competencies.
    _____ F. Accomplish their goals.
    _____ G. Demonstrate their abilities.
    _____ H. Interact with others.

7. When correcting my children's misbehavior, I am usually:

   _____ A. Firm, authoritative, determined, and consistent.

   _____ B. Animated, assertive, flexible, and persuasive.

   _____ C. Non-combative, sympathetic, forgiving, and tolerant.

   _____ D. Calm, rational, evenhanded, and methodical.

8. When my children are struggling, I tend to:

   _____ E. Encourage them to think through the problem.

   _____ F. Provide guidance and direction.

   _____ G. Encourage them to try a different approach.

   _____ H. Offer a listening ear and emotional support.

9. I encourage my children to handle conflicts by:

   _____ A. Standing up for what is right.

   _____ B. Finding a compromise that satisfies everyone.

   _____ C. Understanding the other person's perspective.

   _____ D. Analyzing the situation objectively.

10. I believe it's most important for my children to learn:

   _____ E. Critical thinking and independent decision-making.

   _____ F. The value of hard work and perseverance.

   _____ G. Adaptability and resilience in the face of challenges.

   _____ H. Emotional intelligence and self-awareness.

11. When it comes to rules and boundaries, I:

   _____ A. Set clear expectations and consistent consequences.

   _____ B. Set them but allow for flexibility and adaptability.

   _____ C. Explain the reasons behind them and encourage discussion.

   _____ D. Expect them to be followed but am open to discussion if there's a good reason.

12. I believe the role of a parent is to:

   _____ E. Foster intellectual growth and independence.

   _____ F. Provide structure, guidance, and discipline.

   _____ G. Encourage exploration, creativity, and self-expression.

   _____ H. Provide love, support, and understanding.

13. When it comes to my children's social life, I encourage them to:
    _____ A. Be respectful, considerate, and reliable friends.
    _____ B. Be social, outgoing, and active.
    _____ C. Form deep, meaningful relationships.
    _____ D. Form connections but also maintain their independence.

14. My main goal as a parent is to raise children who are:
    _____ E. Intellectually curious and independent thinkers.
    _____ F. Responsible, disciplined, and productive.
    _____ G. Confident, adaptable, and creative.
    _____ H. Emotionally intelligent and compassionate.

15. I encourage my children to make healthy lifestyle choices by:
    _____ A. Setting routines for meals and disciplined activities.
    _____ B. Engaging in fun and active activities with them.
    _____ C. Discussing the importance of emotional and physical well-being.
    _____ D. Providing information on the benefits of a healthy lifestyle.

16. I help my children develop their values and ethics by:
    - _____ E. Encouraging them to think critically about right and wrong.
    - _____ F. Teaching them the importance of honesty, integrity, and responsibility.
    - _____ G. Encouraging them to stand up for what they believe in.
    - _____ H. Encouraging them to explore their feelings and understand the impact of their actions on others.

17. I foster my children's self esteem and confidence by:
    - _____ A. Setting difficult, but achievable goals, and celebrating their achievements.
    - _____ B. Encouraging them to take on new challenges and believe in their abilities.
    - _____ C. Providing positive reinforcement and acknowledging their efforts.
    - _____ D. Encouraging independent thinking and problem-solving.

18. I teach my children to cope with stress and anxiety by:
    - _____ E. Encouraging them to analyze the situation and develop a plan to address it.
    - _____ F. Teaching them stress-management techniques and the importance of self-care.
    - _____ G. Encouraging them to stay active and engaged in activities that bring them joy.
    - _____ H. Providing a supportive environment and encouraging them to express their feelings.

19. I guide my children on the responsible use of technology and media by:

   _____ A. Setting clear rules and limits on technology and media use.

   _____ B. Encouraging them to balance online activities with outdoor activities and face-to-face interactions.

   _____ C. Discussing the emotional impact of online interactions and content.

   _____ D. Providing information on the potential risks and benefits of technology.

20. My approach to my children's education and continuous learning is:

   _____ E. Encouraging intellectual curiosity and critical thinking.

   _____ F. Structured and organized with clear expectations and goals.

   _____ G. Flexible and adaptive to their interests and passions.

   _____ H. Focused on their emotional and social development as well as academic achievement.

Scoring

Go back and count how many times you chose each letter for all 20 questions. Record that total next to its letter below. Then total up the values in each column. The highest score is the parenting style that is most like you.

C	A	D	B
H	F	E	G
C+H=	A+F=	D+E=	B+G=
Blue	Gold	Green	Orange

Alternative Scoring Method. If you desire, you can also figure out your complete parenting spectrum: the order and value of all four colors in your spectrum. To do that, for each question, rather than choosing the single response that is most like you, rank all of the responses for each question. Give four points to the one that is most like you, three to the next, two to the following, and one point to the response that is the least like you.

Or, if you feel like you tie between two or more responses, or don't have any preferences at all for a particular response, you can also distribute the 10 points across all four responses. This means you can allocate 0 points or identical points if you desire. Then add up the points as before. This is your parenting style spectrum.

If you want to find the percentage of each color, total up the points for all four colors (which should be 200 if you scored properly). Divide the points allocated to each color by the total points and multiply the result by 100 to convert it to a percentage.

Chapter 3

The Blue Parenting Style

Blue parents are known for their compassionate, nurturing, and supportive approach to parenting. In this chapter, we explore the ten key characteristics of the Blue parenting style, from fostering positive relationships and promoting personal growth, to maintaining a harmonious environment and encouraging interaction and socialization.

Blue Parent Summary

1. Emotional Support and Understanding
2. Fostering Positive Relationships
3. Promoting Personal Growth
4. Maintaining a Harmonious Environment
5. Active Participation in Children's Lives
6. Communication and Listening
7. Teaching Important Values
8. Physical Affection and Care
9. Celebrating and Enjoying Life
10. Encouraging Interaction and Socialization

Introduction

Parenting is a journey filled with ups and downs, joys and challenges. For parents who identify with the Blue personality type, parenting is approached with a compassionate, nurturing, and supportive mindset. Blue parents are known for their benevolent nature, desire for harmonious relationships, and emphasis on emotional connection. In this chapter, we will explore the ten key characteristics that define the Blue parenting style, from fostering positive relationships and promoting personal growth, to maintaining a harmonious environment and encouraging interaction and socialization.

1. Emotional Support and Understanding

Blue parents are benevolent and compassionate, always putting the needs of their children first. They understand that children need to be heard and supported, so they make a conscious effort to empathically listen to their children's concerns. For example, if a child is upset about a situation at school, a Blue parent will take the time to sit down, listen, and discuss the child's feelings without judgment. This compassionate approach helps the child feel supported and understood.

Providing comfort when kids are sad or upset is second nature to Blue parents. They are adept at picking up on their children's emotions and will offer a shoulder to cry on or a listening ear whenever it's needed. For instance, if a child is feeling down because they didn't make the sports team, a Blue parent will provide comfort and encouragement, reminding the child of their strengths and encouraging them to try again next time.

Blue parents also show empathy towards their children's struggles. They understand that growing up comes with its challenges, and they make it a point to validate their children's feelings and experiences. For example, if a child is struggling with a subject at school, a Blue parent will acknowledge the difficulty and provide support and encouragement to help the child overcome the challenge.

Providing emotional support and encouragement is a hallmark of Blue parenting. They are always there to cheer their children on, whether it's at a sports event, a school performance, or just in daily life. A Blue parent knows the importance of positive reinforcement and will always try to celebrate their child's achievements, no matter how small.

Affection is also an important aspect of Blue parenting. Blue parents are not afraid to show their love openly, whether it's with a hug, a kiss, or a kind word. They understand the importance of physical touch and make it a point to show their affection regularly. This helps the child feel loved and secure in their relationship with their parents.

2. Fostering Positive Relationships

Blue parents actively seek to bond family members together. They believe that a strong family bond is essential for the well-being of each member. They make it a priority to spend quality time together as a family, whether it's having dinner together, playing games, or going on family outings. For example, a Blue parent might organize a weekly family movie night or a monthly outing to a favorite park. These activities help to foster a sense of belonging and togetherness among family members.

One summer, a Blue parent noticed a growing distance between their teenage daughter and younger son due to their age difference and varied interests. Sensing an opportunity to strengthen their bond, the parent organized a family project: building a treehouse in the backyard. The project not only required collaboration but also tapped into each child's unique skills and interests. The teenager, with her budding architectural inclinations, sketched out the design, while the younger son, an avid nature enthusiast, chose the perfect tree and surrounding decor. Throughout the summer, the entire family worked together, hammering, painting, and decorating. The finished treehouse became a symbol of their combined efforts and shared memories. It provided a space where the siblings could bond over stories, games, and stargazing, bringing them closer than ever before.

Supporting expressions of individuality and creativity is also important to Blue parents. They understand that each family member is unique and should be celebrated for their individuality. They encourage their children to express themselves, whether it's through art, music, or any other creative outlet. For example, if a child shows an interest in painting, a Blue parent will provide the necessary supplies and encourage the child to explore their artistic side.

Helping their children build meaningful relationships is another priority for Blue parents. They understand the importance of social connections and encourage their children to develop strong, healthy relationships with others. They might facilitate playdates, encourage their children to join clubs or sports teams, or simply teach their children the importance of being kind and considerate to others. For example, a Blue parent might encourage their child to invite a new classmate over for a playdate to help them feel welcome.

Valuing quality time spent together as a family is a cornerstone of Blue parenting. Blue parents understand that spending time together as a family helps to strengthen the bond between family members and create lasting memories. They make it a point to prioritize family time, even in the midst of busy schedules. For example, a Blue parent might make it a point to have dinner together as a family every night, even if it means adjusting their work schedule to make it happen.

3. Promoting Personal Growth

Blue parents work diligently to instill a sense of kindness and consideration in their children. They lead by example, demonstrating kindness in their interactions with others and discussing the importance of consideration with their children. A Blue parent might, for example, make a point of showing gratitude to a server at a restaurant, explaining to their child why it's important to be appreciative.

Encouraging the exploration of interests and passions is another way Blue parents promote personal growth. They pay attention to their children's interests and provide opportunities for them to delve deeper into those areas. If a child shows an interest in animals, a Blue parent might take them to the zoo, help them research different species online, or encourage them to read books about animals.

Blue parents also strive to cultivate empathy and compassion in their children. They encourage their children to think about the feelings of others and to show compassion in their interactions. A Blue parent might, for instance, discuss a news story about a natural disaster with their child, encouraging them to think about how the people affected might be feeling and what could be done to help.

Nurturing imagination and expressiveness are also important to Blue parents. They provide opportunities for creative expression and encourage their children to use their imagination in different ways. A Blue parent might provide a variety of art supplies, encourage imaginative play, or support their child in putting on a play or writing a story.

Blue parents value personal growth and encourage their children to engage in self-reflection. They might, for example, have regular conversations with their children about their feelings, thoughts, and experiences, encouraging them to think about what they have learned and how they have grown.

Blue parents are supportive of their children's endeavors, providing encouragement and praise for their efforts. They celebrate their children's achievements, no matter how small, and provide constructive feedback to help them improve. A Blue parent might, for example, attend their child's sports events, applauding their efforts and discussing ways to improve afterwards.

4. Maintaining a Harmonious Environment

Blue parents strive to create a supportive and nurturing home environment where every family member feels loved and valued. They make a conscious effort to create a warm and welcoming atmosphere in their home. This might involve creating cozy spaces for relaxation, having open conversations about each family member's needs and feelings, and making sure everyone feels heard and respected.

Running the household democratically is another way Blue parents maintain a harmonious environment. They involve all family members in decision-making processes, valuing each person's opinion and fostering a sense of shared responsibility. This might involve having family meetings to discuss plans, solve problems, or make decisions together.

One evening, as thunder rumbled outside, the power went out in the Blue household. Instead of letting frustration take over, the Blue parents turned this situation into an opportunity for family bonding. They gathered everyone in the living room, lighting candles and distributing blankets. The family then began sharing stories from their day, with each person taking a turn. The youngest child expressed frustration about a toy she couldn't share with her sister, while the eldest spoke about a challenge he faced in school. With the guidance of the Blue parents, each situation was discussed, solutions proposed, and affirmations exchanged. The evening transformed from a potential source of stress into a heartwarming memory of togetherness and mutual support. The power outage, rather than being a disruption, became an emblem of the harmonious environment that Blue parents ardently foster.

Valuing the contributions of each family member is also important to Blue parents. They make a point of acknowledging and appreciating the efforts of each family member, regardless of how small. This might involve expressing gratitude for everyday acts of kindness, celebrating each other's achievements, or acknowledging each other's efforts in maintaining the household.

Blue parents prioritize open communication to prevent arguments and fighting between children. They teach their children how to express their feelings and resolve conflicts in a constructive manner. For instance, they might guide their children in having a conversation about a disagreement, helping them to understand each other's perspectives and find a mutually agreeable solution.

Keeping the peace in the household is a consistent effort for Blue parents. They strive to create a calm and peaceful atmosphere, where conflicts are addressed promptly and amicably. This involves mediating any emerging disputes between family members, encouraging transparent communication, and fostering a positive, supportive attitude towards one another.

5. Active Participation in Children's Lives

Blue parents have a strong desire to be at home as much as possible to be actively involved in their children's lives. They prioritize spending time with their children over other commitments and make a conscious effort to be present both physically and emotionally. This might involve rearranging their work schedule, reducing social commitments, or finding ways to work from home to spend more time with their children.

Attending their children's games, concerts, and performances is another way Blue parents show their active involvement. They try to be present at their children's activities, showing their support and encouragement. Whether it's a school play, a soccer game, or a music recital, Blue parents are there to cheer their children on.

Taking their children to artistic and cultural events is also important for Blue parents. They see value in exposing their children to a variety of experiences and encourage them to appreciate art, music, and culture. This might involve visiting museums, attending concerts, or participating in cultural festivals.

Blue parents want to be intimately involved in their children's lives. They take an interest in their children's activities, thoughts, and feelings, and make an effort to understand their world. This might involve having regular one-on-one time with each child, asking open-ended questions about their day, and showing genuine interest in their thoughts and feelings.

6. Communication and Listening

Promoting open communication and dialog is a key priority for Blue parents. They create an environment where their children feel comfortable expressing their thoughts and feelings without fear of judgment or criticism. This might involve setting aside dedicated time for family discussions, actively listening to their children's perspectives, and sharing their own thoughts and feelings in an open and honest manner.

Enjoying talking with family around the kitchen table is a cherished activity for Blue parents. They value the simple act of spending time together as a family, sharing stories, and discussing the events of the day. This might involve making a conscious effort to have meals together as a family, without distractions like television or smartphones, and using this time to connect with each other.

Listening attentively to their children's thoughts and feelings is another important aspect of communication for Blue parents. They try to understand their children's perspectives and show empathy towards their experiences. This might involve actively listening without interrupting, asking clarifying questions, and validating their children's feelings.

Valuing and respecting their children's opinions is crucial for Blue parents. They encourage their children to express their thoughts and opinions, even if they differ from their own, and show respect by considering their perspectives. This might involve actively seeking their children's input on family decisions, acknowledging their viewpoints, and finding ways to incorporate their ideas into the decision-making process.

7. Teaching Important Values

Teaching their children the importance of teamwork and cooperation is a vital value for Blue parents. They often engage their children in activities that require collaboration and mutual support. For instance, they might organize family games that require team effort, or encourage their children to participate in group activities or sports that foster a sense of community and cooperation.

Instilling a sense of gratitude in their children is another key value for Blue parents. They often model gratitude by expressing thankfulness for the blessings in their life and encourage their children to do the same. For example, they might make it a habit to share something they are grateful for at the end of each day and encourage their children to do the same.

Coaching their children on the importance of giving and helping others is a core value for Blue parents. They often involve their children in acts of kindness and charity, such as volunteering at a local shelter or donating to a food bank. They might also encourage their children to think of ways they can help others in their daily lives, such as helping a neighbor with groceries or supporting a friend in need.

Teaching their children the importance of empathy and understanding others' feelings is another crucial value for Blue parents. They often have conversations with their children about the importance of putting themselves in others' shoes and considering their feelings. They might also encourage their children to reflect on how their actions might affect others and to show kindness and compassion in their interactions.

Encouraging their children to actively participate in community service and helping others is another key value for Blue parents. They often involve their children in volunteering opportunities and encourage them to take an active role in making a positive impact in their community. For example, they might participate in a community clean-up day as a family, or encourage their children to organize a fund-raiser for a cause they care about.

8. Physical Affection and Care

Blue parents give their hearts and souls to their children, always prioritizing their children's needs and well-being above all else. They often go out of their way to ensure their children feel loved, supported, and cared for in every possible way. Whether it's staying up late to help with a school project, or spending quality time together on the weekends, Blue parents are always there for their children.

Placing their children's needs before housework, spouse, or self is another characteristic of Blue parents. They often rearrange their schedules or put off their own needs to ensure their children's needs are met. For example, a Blue parent might delay their own plans to ensure their child has a ride to a friend's house or has help with their homework.

Blue parents also try to anticipate their children's emotional needs. They are often attuned to their children's moods and feelings and try to provide support before it is even asked for. For example, if they notice their child seems down or upset, they might initiate a conversation to check in on how they are feeling and offer a listening ear.

To illustrate, consider this story. One chilly winter morning, Mia, a 10-year-old, woke up feeling under the weather. Noticing her subdued demeanor, her Blue parent immediately sprang into action. The regular hustle of preparing for work was momentarily put on pause. Instead, the living room was transformed into a cozy cocoon with blankets, hot chocolate, and Mia's favorite movies lined up. As she nestled into the warmth, her parent joined her, holding her close, letting the rhythmic beats of their hearts sync. There were no words spoken, just the silent affirmation of unwavering love and care. For Mia, that day wasn't about being sick; it became a cherished memory of being enveloped in the warmth of her parent's undying affection.

Blue parents use lots of physical touch to show affection to their children. They often hug, kiss, and cuddle their children to show them how much they are loved. Physical affection is an important way for Blue parents to express their love and create a strong bond with their children.

9. Celebrating and Enjoying Life

Blue parents enjoy watching shows, even cartoons, with their children. They see it as an opportunity to bond and share a laugh with their kids. It's not just about the activity, but the quality time spent together. Whether it's a new movie or a favorite cartoon series, watching shows together is a cherished activity for Blue parents and their children.

Making a big deal of holidays, birthdays, and anniversaries is another characteristic of Blue parents. They often go above and beyond to make these occasions special and memorable for their children. Whether it's decorating the house, baking a favorite cake, or planning a surprise party, Blue parents put in the effort to make these moments special.

Weekend picnics are a favorite tradition for many Blue families. On sunny days, they often pack a basket full of homemade treats, grab a colorful blanket, and venture to a local park or lakeside. There, amidst nature, they revel in simple pleasures—the melody of birds, the gentle rustle of leaves, and the joyous laughter of children playing. Parents and kids alike participate in games, share stories, and savor delicious food. It's not just about the picnic; it's about celebrating the beauty of life, cherishing the present, and creating memories that will be treasured for years to come.

Blue parents also want to see the family do things together. They believe that spending quality time together as a family strengthens the bond between family members. Whether it's going for a walk, playing a board game, or cooking a meal together, Blue parents value the time spent together as a family.

Blue parents pride themselves on "caring" more than other parents. They often go above and beyond to show their love and support for their children. Whether it's attending every school event, helping with homework, or providing a listening ear, Blue parents make it a priority to show their children how much they care.

10. Encouraging Interaction and Socialization

Blue parents often chat with their children about their friends and activities. They show genuine interest in their children's social lives and the things that matter to them. By engaging in conversations about their friends and activities, Blue parents show their children that they value their opinions and experiences.

Blue parents also look to popular, public experts for advice. They are always seeking to improve their parenting skills and often turn to trusted experts for guidance. Whether it's reading books, attending seminars, or following parenting blogs, Blue parents are proactive about seeking advice and learning new strategies to support their children.

Patience and understanding are key qualities of Blue parents. They understand that children are constantly learning and growing, and they approach parenting challenges with a patient and understanding attitude. Whether it's navigating a toddler tantrum or dealing with a moody teenager, Blue parents approach each situation with empathy and a desire to understand their child's perspective.

Blue parents provide a safe space for their children to express themselves. They create an environment where their children feel comfortable sharing their thoughts, feelings, and concerns. Whether it's a casual conversation at the dinner table or a more serious discussion about a problem at school, Blue parents make it a priority to create a safe and supportive space for their children to express themselves.

Review

The Blue parenting style is characterized by its compassionate, supportive, and nurturing approach. Blue parents seek to foster positive relationships, promote personal growth, and maintain a harmonious environment for their children. They actively participate in their children's lives, communicate openly, and teach important values. Additionally, they show physical affection and care, celebrate life's joys, and encourage interaction and socialization. While parenting is never a one-size-fits-all approach, understanding the characteristics of the Blue parenting style can provide valuable insights and strategies for those who identify with this personality type.

Blue Parent Checklist

☐ Are benevolent and compassionate parents.

☐ Desire a supportive, nurturing home environment.

☐ Run the household democratically.

☐ Value the contributions of each family member.

☐ Foster a sense of kindness and consideration in their children.

☐ Give their hearts and souls to their children.

☐ Seek to bond family members together.

☐ Support expressions of individuality and creativity.

☐ Try to fulfill their children's desires.

☐ Want to be at home as much as possible.

☐ Dislike arguments and fighting between children.

☐ Take their children to artistic, cultural events.

☐ Keep the peace in the household.

☐ Attend their children's games, concerts, performances.

☐ Empathically listen to their children's concerns.

☐ Help their children feel good about themselves.

☐ Mirror the emotions of their children.

☐ Place kids' needs before housework, spouse, self.

☐ Provide comfort when kids are sad or upset.

☐ Try to anticipate their kids' emotional needs.

☐ Want to be intimately involved in their children's lives.

☐ Use lots of physical touch to show affection.

☐ Promote open communication and dialog.

☐ Enjoy talking with family around the kitchen table.

☐ Enjoy watching shows, even cartoons, with kids.

☐ Look to popular, public experts for advice.

- ☐ Make a big deal of holidays, birthdays, anniversaries.
- ☐ Want to see the family do things together.
- ☐ Pride themselves on "caring" more than other parents.
- ☐ Chat with children about friends and activities.
- ☐ Show empathy towards their children's struggles.
- ☐ Listen attentively to their children's thoughts and feelings.
- ☐ Value and respect their children's opinions.
- ☐ Are patient and understanding.
- ☐ Provide a safe space for their children to express themselves.
- ☐ Support the exploration of their children's interests and passions.
- ☐ Provide emotional support and encouragement.
- ☐ Are affectionate and show their love openly.
- ☐ Cultivate empathy and compassion in their children.
- ☐ Value harmony and work towards resolving conflicts peacefully.
- ☐ Teach their children the importance of teamwork and cooperation.
- ☐ Nurture their children's imagination and expressiveness.
- ☐ Value personal growth and encourage their children to self-reflect.
- ☐ Are supportive of their children's endeavors.
- ☐ Help their children build meaningful relationships.
- ☐ Value quality time spent together as a family.
- ☐ Instill a sense of gratitude in their children.
- ☐ Teach their children the importance of giving and helping others.

- ☐ Teach their children the importance of empathy and understanding others' feelings.
- ☐ Encourage their children to actively participate in community service and helping others.

Chapter 4

The Gold Parenting Style

Explore the world of Gold parents, who are known for their structured approach to parenting, emphasizing responsibility, respect, and community involvement. This chapter delves into the ten key characteristics that define Gold parents, from promoting financial literacy to teaching the importance of hard work and perseverance.

Gold Parent Summary

1. Promoting Responsibility and Accountability
2. Fostering Respect and Politeness
3. Valuing Tradition and Heritage
4. Ensuring Safety and Security
5. Encouraging Leadership and Achievement
6. Instilling Organizational Skills
7. Teaching the Importance of Time Management
8. Promoting Community Involvement
9. Prioritizing Education
10. Emphasizing Self-reliance and Independence

Introduction

Dive into the realm of Gold parents, a group distinguished by their emphasis on instilling organizational skills, prioritizing education, and fostering respect and politeness. This chapter offers a detailed look into the fundamental principles that shape the philosophy of Gold parents. From valuing tradition and heritage to ensuring safety and security for their children, we will explore the top 10 core values and practices that guide their parenting approach.

1. Promoting Responsibility and Accountability

Helping children set and achieve meaningful goals is a key aspect of being a Gold parent. This not only involves guiding them in identifying their objectives but also in breaking these down into manageable tasks and monitoring progress. For instance, if a child expresses a desire to improve their grades, a Gold parent might help them develop a study schedule, identify areas for improvement, and regularly check-in on their progress. This approach instills a sense of responsibility in the child, as they learn the importance of setting goals and working diligently to achieve them.

Ensuring chores and homework are completed before playtime is another way Gold parents instill responsibility in their children. This teaches them the importance of prioritizing their responsibilities and fulfilling their obligations before engaging in leisure activities. A Gold parent might establish a routine where the child is expected to complete their homework and household chores immediately after school before they are allowed to play with friends or engage in other recreational activities. Over time, this helps the child develop a strong work ethic and an understanding of the importance of fulfilling their responsibilities.

Requiring children to perform household chores regularly is another characteristic of Gold parents. This not only teaches them essential life skills but also fosters a sense of responsibility and contribution to the household. A Gold parent might assign specific chores to each family member and expect them to be completed thoroughly and on time. This could involve creating a weekly chore chart and rotating the tasks among family members. This approach not only ensures the fair distribution of household responsibilities but also teaches the child the importance of contributing to the household and working as a team.

Expecting children to be accountable for their actions is a crucial aspect of Gold parenting. This involves holding them responsible for their behavior, both positive and negative, and helping them understand the consequences of their actions. If a child behaves inappropriately, a Gold parent will address the issue directly and discuss the impact of their actions on others. Similarly, positive behavior is acknowledged and praised, reinforcing the child's understanding of the importance of behaving responsibly and considerately.

Teaching the importance of self-discipline is another key aspect of Gold parenting. This involves helping the child develop the ability to control their impulses and make decisions that are in their best interest. For instance, a Gold parent might help their child develop a daily routine that includes time for homework, chores, and leisure activities. This helps the child learn the importance of managing their time effectively and making choices that contribute to their well-being and success.

Encouraging the development of a strong work ethic is another characteristic of Gold parents. This involves instilling in the child the importance of working hard, being diligent, and persevering in the face of challenges. A Gold parent might emphasize the importance of completing tasks to the best of their ability and not giving up when faced with difficulties. This could involve providing support and encouragement when the child is struggling, while also emphasizing the importance of persistence and effort.

Planning for the future is another important value that Gold parents instill in their children. They often have conversations with their children about their goals and aspirations and provide guidance and support in developing a plan to achieve them. A Gold parent might sit down with their child to discuss their interests and strengths, for example, and help them to identify potential career paths or educational opportunities. They might also discuss the importance of setting goals and developing a plan to achieve them. This approach not only fosters a sense of self-awareness and ambition but also instills in their children the importance of planning for the future.

2. Fostering Respect and Politeness

Gold parents understand the importance of instilling a sense of respect and politeness in their children from a young age. They believe that these qualities are fundamental to building strong relationships and achieving success in life. Therefore, they expect their children to show respect and politeness to their elders and others in their community. For example, a Gold parent might remind their child to greet their grandparents warmly, express gratitude for gifts or kindness, and listen attentively when an elder is speaking.

Insisting on proper manners and etiquette is also a cornerstone of Gold parenting. Gold parents believe that knowing how to behave appropriately in various social situations is crucial for their children's development and future success. This includes not only using polite language and gestures but also understanding and respecting the customs and traditions of others. For example, a Gold parent might teach their child the importance of sending thank-you notes after receiving gifts, or the appropriate way to greet someone in a different culture.

Promoting respectfulness and courtesy in their children is another key aspect of Gold parenting. Gold parents believe that being respectful and courteous to others is not only the right thing to do but also helps to build strong, positive relationships. Therefore, they actively encourage their children to be considerate of others' feelings, to listen attentively, and to express their thoughts and opinions respectfully. For example, a Gold parent might encourage their child to consider how their actions might affect others and to think before they speak or act.

Teaching the importance of honor and integrity is also fundamental to Gold parenting. They believe that having a strong moral compass is essential for their children's development and well-being. Therefore, they teach their children the importance of being honest, trustworthy, and doing the right thing, even when it is difficult. For example, a Gold parent might discuss with their child the importance of admitting when they have made a mistake and taking responsibility for their actions.

3. Valuing Tradition and Heritage

Gold parents understand the importance of preserving their family's legacy and take great pride in their family name, heritage, and traditions. They believe that honoring their past and passing down family values to their children helps instill a sense of identity and belonging. This might involve sharing family stories, celebrating cultural traditions, or maintaining connections with extended family members. For instance, a Gold parent might organize a family reunion, share stories about their ancestors, or teach their child a traditional recipe that has been passed down through generations.

Valuing tradition and passing down family values is central to the Gold parenting approach. Gold parents believe that instilling a strong sense of values in their children will guide them in making good decisions throughout their lives. This includes teaching them about the importance of honesty, integrity, hard work, and respect for others. A Gold parent might involve their children in family traditions or rituals that reflect these values, or have conversations with them about the reasons behind their family's customs and beliefs.

Creating family mission statements and goals is another way Gold parents instill a sense of purpose and direction in their children. They believe that having a clear set of shared goals helps to unite the family and gives each member a sense of responsibility and accountability. This might involve sitting down as a family to discuss and agree on a set of shared values, goals, and expectations, and then finding ways to work towards them together. For instance, a Gold parent might facilitate a family discussion about the importance of community service and then involve the whole family in volunteering activities.

4. Ensuring Safety and Security

Providing a secure and safe home environment is of utmost importance to Gold parents. They believe that creating a stable and predictable environment helps their children feel safe and supported. This might involve setting clear boundaries and rules, maintaining a consistent routine, and taking measures to ensure their children's physical safety. For example, a Gold parent might install safety gates or locks, regularly check in with their children to make sure they are safe, or establish clear guidelines about acceptable behavior both online and offline.

Closely monitoring their children is another way Gold parents ensure their safety and well-being. They believe that by keeping a watchful eye on their children's activities, friendships, and whereabouts, they can protect them from potential dangers and negative influences. This might involve checking their children's social media accounts, having open conversations about their friends and activities, or setting guidelines about where they can go and who they can spend time with. A Gold parent might ask their child about their plans for the day, who they will be with, and when they will be home.

Requiring pre-approval of friends and activities is another way Gold parents maintain control over their children's environment. They believe that by knowing who their children are spending time with and what they are doing, they can ensure that they are making good choices and staying safe. This might involve meeting their children's friends and their parents, asking questions about planned activities, or setting guidelines about acceptable and unacceptable activities. A Gold parent might ask to meet a new friend's parents before allowing their child to go to their house, or set clear guidelines about acceptable activities and places to go.

5. Encouraging Leadership and Achievement

Gold parents are deeply invested in guiding their children toward success. They see their role as not just nurturers but as coaches, identifying their children's strengths and weaknesses and pushing them to excel. A Gold parent might enroll their child in specialized courses or extracurricular activities that align with their skills, constantly seeking opportunities that could serve as stepping stones to future success. They often set the bar high, not to exert pressure, but to instill the value of ambition and hard work.

When it comes to expectations, Gold parents don't just want their children to meet them; they want them to exceed them. These parents might establish clearly defined goals for their children—be it academic achievement, sports performance, or community involvement—and provide the resources and support to help them surpass these objectives. When a Gold parent says, "You can do better," it's often a motivational mantra, urging their children to go above and beyond in all their endeavors.

Leadership is a quality highly valued by Gold parents, and they actively encourage their children to take on roles that cultivate this skill. Whether it's running for student council, captaining a sports team, or spearheading a community project, they view these experiences as crucial for personal development. A Gold parent might coach their child on public speaking, decision-making, and the nuances of effective leadership, reinforcing the idea that these skills are invaluable both now and in the future.

Having high expectations for their children's achievements comes naturally to Gold parents. They are often their children's biggest cheerleaders but also their most constructive critics. They celebrate wins, big or small, but also turn setbacks into teachable moments. By setting a high standard for achievement, Gold parents believe they are preparing their children for the challenges and opportunities that lie ahead, instilling in them a drive for excellence that will serve them well throughout their lives.

6. Instilling Organizational Skills

Gold parents understand that managing finances is a critical life skill, and they often involve their children in the process of creating and managing household budgets. They may sit down as a family to discuss expenses, savings goals, and financial planning, teaching their children the importance of being fiscally responsible from a young age. A Gold parent might also involve their child in comparing prices at the grocery store or planning a budget for a family outing, turning everyday tasks into valuable learning experiences.

Methodical planning is a hallmark of Gold parents, extending to all aspects of family life, from grocery shopping to weekend outings. They often involve their children in the planning process, teaching them the importance of foresight and preparation. A Gold parent might create a checklist for a family picnic, assigning each family member a task and discussing the reasoning behind each decision. This not only ensures a successful outing but also instills in their children the value of planning and organization.

For Gold parents, doing tasks in the proper way, order, and time is non-negotiable. They often create routines and schedules to ensure that household tasks and responsibilities are completed efficiently. A Gold parent might create a weekly chore chart, for example, assigning specific tasks to each family member and discussing the importance of each chore in maintaining a harmonious home. This approach not only fosters a sense of responsibility in their children but also teaches them the importance of time management and organization.

A well-organized bedroom is often a point of emphasis for Gold parents. They believe that a tidy and organized living space is essential for mental clarity and productivity. A Gold parent might work with their child to create a system for organizing toys, clothes, and other belongings, discussing the importance of keeping things in their proper place. Regular check-ins and gentle reminders help reinforce these habits, ultimately instilling in their children a sense of pride in maintaining an orderly living space.

Taking good care of one's possessions is a value that Gold parents instill in their children from a young age. They often use personal anecdotes or stories to illustrate the consequences of neglecting one's belongings. For example, a Gold parent might share a story about a cherished possession that was lost or damaged due to carelessness, highlighting the importance of treating one's belongings with care and respect.

7. Teaching the Importance of Time Management

Punctuality is highly valued by Gold parents, and they often set clear expectations for mealtimes and other activities. Being on time is seen as a sign of respect and consideration for others. A Gold parent might establish a set dinner time, for example, and discuss the importance of being punctual with their children. They may explain that when everyone is on time, the meal can be enjoyed while it is hot, and everyone can share their day's experiences together.

Discipline is administered firmly and consistently by Gold parents. They believe that clear and consistent boundaries are essential for a child's development. A Gold parent might establish a set of household rules and discuss the consequences of breaking them with their children. For example, if a child fails to complete their chores on time, they might lose privileges such as screen time. This approach not only fosters a sense of responsibility but also teaches children the importance of consequences and accountability.

Gold parents often focus on household tasks without getting sidetracked. They believe in setting a good example for their children by completing tasks efficiently and effectively. A Gold parent might create a to-do list for the day and involve their children in completing the tasks. For example, they might assign their child the task of setting the table while they prepare dinner. This approach not only fosters a sense of teamwork but also teaches children the importance of focus and efficiency.

8. Promoting Community Involvement

Gold parents believe in the importance of giving back to the community and often promote volunteering at school. They view volunteering as an opportunity for their children to develop a sense of responsibility, empathy, and a strong work ethic. A Gold parent might encourage their child to join a school-based service club or to participate in service activities organized by the school. Or they might encourage their child to participate in a local clean-up event or to volunteer at a local food bank. They might also discuss the importance of community service and the positive impact it can have on both the individual and the community. This approach not only fosters a sense of responsibility and empathy but also instills in their children the importance of contributing to the community.

Beyond mere participation, Gold parents often lead by example, actively engaging in community activities themselves. They believe that children learn best by observing the actions of those they look up to. Therefore, it's not uncommon to find Gold parents taking on leadership roles in neighborhood associations, school PTA meetings, or volunteering in local charity events. They might organize neighborhood garage sales for a cause, participate in tree-planting days, or lead a team in charity walks. By doing so, they not only show their children the value of service but also offer them firsthand experience in teamwork, leadership, and project management.

Additionally, these experiences in community involvement can often lead to significant teachable moments for the Gold parent. After participating in community events, they might sit down with their children to reflect on the day's activities, discussing the challenges faced, the benefits of teamwork, and the joy of seeing the direct results of one's efforts. These debriefing sessions are invaluable as they deepen the child's understanding of the activity and reinforce the virtues of perseverance, collaboration, and the intrinsic rewards of service. In this way, Gold parents ensure that the lessons learned during community involvement are internalized and remembered, shaping their children's character for years to come.

9. Prioritizing Education

Gold parents place immense value on education, consistently encouraging academic excellence in their offspring. They set clear academic expectations, ensuring that their children have the necessary resources and environments conducive to learning. For instance, a Gold parent might design a serene and organized study space, or offer extra educational materials and tutoring when required. They emphasize the long-term benefits of a robust education, making it clear that it lays the foundation for a promising future. Their guidance not only instills dedication and ambition but also drives home the significance of prioritizing education.

Alongside academic prowess, Gold parents believe in the importance of honoring school-related commitments. They engage in discussions with their children about the necessity of being consistent with school projects, homework deadlines, and other educational responsibilities. A Gold parent might delve into the consequences of neglecting such duties, stressing its repercussions on academic performance and personal growth. The emphasis here is on cultivating reliability, especially in the educational sphere.

Furthermore, in the context of education, Gold parents also underline the relevance of loyalty and trustworthiness. For instance, when it comes to group projects or team research, staying loyal to one's responsibilities and being trustworthy in collaborations becomes vital. Gold parents might highlight scenarios where these values are compromised and the subsequent impact on academic endeavors. Their teachings aim to inculcate integrity, emphasizing that it goes hand-in-hand with academic success.

10. Emphasizing Self-reliance and Independence

Gold parents champion financial independence, ensuring their children understand the nuances of money management. For instance, they might initiate discussions about earning an allowance through chores, the wisdom of saving for a coveted toy, or the significance of budgeting for a school trip. Highlighting stories of those who faced hardships due to poor financial decisions, they underline the essence of monetary self-reliance. Their lessons transcend mere financial literacy, molding their children into individuals who appreciate the freedom and empowerment stemming from fiscal responsibility.

Embodying the essence of self-reliance, Gold parents prioritize equipping their children with the skills to stand on their own. They might share anecdotes of times they fixed a home appliance without professional help or navigated a challenging situation without external intervention. Through such stories, they underscore the value of self-sufficiency, emphasizing how relying excessively on others can lead to lost opportunities or feelings of helplessness. Their teachings inspire confidence, preparing their children to face challenges head-on without undue dependencies.

Responsibility within the household is another cornerstone of their teachings. Instead of mere directives, they might share a story of a family that thrived due to collective effort or a tale of a sibling duo coordinating to manage the home in their parents' absence. Highlighting the joy of collaboration and the shared pride in a well-maintained home, they inspire their children to actively participate in household chores, fostering both responsibility and a sense of belonging.

Setting a gold standard, quite literally, Gold parents showcase the importance of reliability, perseverance, and leading by example. They might narrate tales of individuals who rose to prominence through sheer determination or instances where dependability turned the tide in challenging situations. By highlighting the pitfalls of laxity or inconsistency, they inspire their children to remain steadfast, emphasizing that in reliability and hard work lie the twin pillars of respect and success.

Review

Gold parents are the architects of the future, shaping their children with the values of responsibility, respect, and self-reliance. They understand the importance of community involvement, education, and setting a good example. While their approach may seem strict and structured, it is grounded in a deep desire to prepare their children for the challenges ahead. Ultimately, Gold parents seek to provide a strong foundation for their children, equipping them with the skills and values necessary to thrive in the world.

Gold Parent Checklist

- ☐ Promote the importance of earning and saving money.
- ☐ Require their children to perform household chores regularly.
- ☐ Drive their children towards success.
- ☐ Urge their children to exceed expectations.
- ☐ Help children set and achieve meaningful goals.
- ☐ Ensure chores and homework are completed before playtime.
- ☐ Seek advice from established authorities or professionals.
- ☐ Are self-reliant and don't see the need for outside interference.
- ☐ Promote volunteering at school.
- ☐ Expect their children to show respect and politeness to elders.
- ☐ Insist on proper manners and etiquette from their children.
- ☐ Teach their children the correct and appropriate actions.
- ☐ Provide a secure and safe home environment.
- ☐ Strictly observe and enforce rules and laws.
- ☐ Closely monitor their children.
- ☐ Exhort their children to persevere until the end.
- ☐ Require pre-approval of friends and activities.
- ☐ Manage household budgets and finances.
- ☐ Plan family activities methodically.
- ☐ Need tasks to be done in the proper way, order, and time.
- ☐ Prefer orderly and well-organized bedrooms.

- ☐ Require their children to take good care of their possessions.
- ☐ Establish family schedules, assignments, and deadlines.
- ☐ Expect punctuality for meals and activities.
- ☐ Administer discipline firmly and consistently.
- ☐ Create family mission statements and goals.
- ☐ Focus on household tasks without getting side-tracked.
- ☐ Maintain a tidy home and run a disciplined household.
- ☐ Take pride in their family name, heritage, and traditions.
- ☐ Consider their children's failures as their own.
- ☐ Emphasize the importance of responsibility and duty.
- ☐ Encourage their children to take on leadership roles.
- ☐ Have high expectations for their children's achievements.
- ☐ Value tradition and passing down family values.
- ☐ Encourage their children to be organized and prepared.
- ☐ Believe in the importance of structure and routine.
- ☐ Teach their children the value of hard work and perseverance.
- ☐ Promote respectfulness and courtesy in their children.
- ☐ Believe in the importance of being reliable and dependable.
- ☐ Teach their children the importance of honor and integrity.
- ☐ Expect their children to contribute to the household.
- ☐ Promote community service involvement in their children.
- ☐ Value education and promote academic excellence.
- ☐ Expect their children to honor their commitments.

- ☐ Teach their children the importance of loyalty and trustworthiness.
- ☐ Encourage their children to plan for the future.
- ☐ Believe in the importance of setting a good example for their children.
- ☐ Expect their children to be accountable for their actions.
- ☐ Teach their children the importance of self-discipline.
- ☐ Encourage their children to develop a strong work ethic.

Chapter 5

The Green Parenting Style

Explore the world of Green parenting and delve deep into strategies designed to foster intellectual growth, critical thinking, emotional stability, and resilience in your children. Uncover the foundational key principles of this transformative approach and get practical, insightful tips to seamlessly implement them in your enriching parenting journey.

Green Parent Summary

1. Fostering Independence and Critical Thinking
2. Encouraging Intellectual and Personal Growth
3. Promoting Creativity and Innovation
4. Openness to Feedback and Adaptability
5. Emotional Stability and Objectivity
6. Encouraging Self-Improvement
7. Enjoying Intellectual Stimulation
8. Promoting Responsibility and Problem Solving
9. Having a Strategic Approach
10. Valuing Knowledge and Understanding

Introduction

Green parenting is a unique approach to raising children that values intellectual development, critical thinking, and emotional stability. It emphasizes the importance of fostering curiosity, promoting self-directed learning, and encouraging independence. This approach does not focus solely on academic achievement, but rather on the development of the whole child—emotionally, socially, and intellectually. In this chapter, we will explore the top 10 key principles of Green parenting and provide practical tips on how to implement them in your own parenting journey.

1. Fostering Independence and Critical Thinking

Green parents emphasize the cultivation of autonomy and individual thought. Recognizing the intrinsic value of self-directed exploration, they establish a safe environment that champions curiosity. Instead of offering pre-packaged knowledge, they present their children with tools and frameworks, empowering them to navigate their own cognitive pathways.

Central to the Green parenting approach is the advocacy for self-driven decision-making. Rather than steering every facet of their child's journey, they provide the scaffolding, ensuring their children comprehend the ramifications of their choices. This not only instills independence but serves as fertile ground for the development of robust critical thinking abilities.

Rather than an elaborate web of rules, Green parents lean towards imparting fundamental principles that inform sound decision-making. They instill the belief that grasping the essence, the "why" behind behaviors, is pivotal, rather than a mere compliance with instructions. By internalizing these foundational principles, their children cultivate an intrinsic moral compass, enabling them to navigate complex scenarios confidently.

Understanding that errors are inevitable—and often enlightening—stages of growth, Green parents refrain from overprotecting. Instead, they see the value in natural consequences, leveraging these instances as potent teaching moments. Through reflection on missteps, children glean insights into better future choices.

Conversations in a Green household are often peppered with probing questions, intended to ignite deeper introspection and analysis. Rather than being accusatory, these questions challenge the child to examine their actions and decisions from varied angles, fostering a multi-dimensional understanding of situations.

Every decision, every strategy Green parents employ is a product of meticulous reflection. They ensure they've considered potential implications, especially as they pertain to their child's holistic development. Such a deliberative stance not only results in well-thought-out parenting choices but offers a model of decision-making excellence for their young ones.

In essence, the core of Green parenting lies in nurturing free thinkers, individuals who aren't shackled by convention but are empowered to think critically and carve out their distinct path. Through encouragement, guidance, and strategic questioning, they're shaping the next generation of independent thinkers and problem solvers.

2. Encouraging Intellectual and Personal Growth

For Green parents, cultivating a deep-rooted sense of curiosity within their children is paramount. They understand that the spark of inquiry is the cornerstone of intellectual development. By offering riveting literature, arranging museum visits, or simply fostering an atmosphere where questions are celebrated, they pave the way for unending exploration.

The essence of critical thought isn't lost on Green parents. They champion the idea that navigating our multifaceted world requires a discerning mind. By prompting their children to analyze, dissect, and evaluate information, they are shaping discerning individuals capable of drawing conclusions rooted in evidence and reason.

By challenging prevailing notions and encouraging their children to do the same, Green parents instill a sense of discernment. This approach isn't about fostering rebellion, but rather nurturing an understanding that acceptance isn't obligatory, especially when it comes to ideas and beliefs. In so doing, they lay the foundation for their children to not only grasp deeper truths but also become catalysts for constructive change.

Opportunities that propel intellectual advancement are always on a Green parent's radar. From promoting extracurricular engagements and participation in intellectual contests to offering access to cutting-edge e-learning platforms, these parents spare no effort in widening their children's horizons.

Shying away from intricate topics isn't the Green way. Instead, they broach profound subjects head-on, fostering dialogues that might be complex but are always enlightening. By teaching their children the art of respectful disagreement, they are shaping future thought leaders capable of nuanced discourse.

In the Green household, logical deliberation holds a prized spot. Children are not just taught to find solutions but are mentored in systematic problem-solving, clear articulation, and robust argumentation—skills they recognize as pivotal for all facets of life.

Knowledge, in the eyes of Green parents, isn't just about accumulation but about depth and application. They rally behind their children's unique pursuits, fostering a culture where diving deep into subjects of passion isn't just encouraged, but celebrated.

The intellectual landscape in a Green parent's abode is nothing short of stimulating. Every corner, every conversation is tailored to push boundaries and redefine norms. Be it through intricate puzzles, nuanced debates, or channels of creative expression, the objective remains clear: nurturing minds that can pivot, adapt, and innovate.

3. Promoting Creativity and Innovation

Green parents instill in their children the value of forging their own path. Rather than merely mirroring societal norms, these parents inspire their offspring to critically assess prevalent beliefs and sculpt their own set of values. Through this, they aim to foster a resilient individuality in their children, enabling them to contribute distinctively to the societal tapestry.

To Green parents, the canvases of creativity and innovation are limitless. In an ever-evolving world, the ability to conjure novel ideas and rethink conventional paradigms is indispensable. Whether it's through visual arts, harmonious melodies, evocative prose, or other imaginative avenues, Green parents are steadfast champions of their children's artistic and inventive pursuits.

Problem-solving, in the Green household, isn't a skill; it's an art. Green parents cultivate an environment where their children aren't just problem solvers but innovative thinkers. While they stand ready to guide, they emphasize the importance of individual analysis, perspective evaluation, and tailored solutions, empowering their children to take the reins of challenges they face.

Embracing diversity of thought is a hallmark of Green parenting. In a multifaceted world, understanding and valuing divergent views is key. By fostering open-mindedness, they equip their children with the tools to synthesize a broader, more enriched world view, enhancing their decision-making prowess.

Conventional wisdom isn't taken at face value in a Green home. Here, children are taught the vitality of probing established norms and pondering unconventional narratives. Such an approach is not about contrarianism but about fostering an in-depth, multifaceted understanding of intricate subjects.

Emotion has its place, but Green parents advocate for a rational and objective lens when it comes to critical decisions. They mentor their children to dissect issues with clear-headedness, basing conclusions on empirical evidence and cogent reasoning, laying the groundwork for judicious choices in life.

Green parents propel their children to aim skyward. The philosophy isn't just about goal-setting, but about crafting intellectually stimulating aspirations. While these parents offer a supportive scaffold, they underscore the significance of their children's agency in crafting their ambitions and reveling in their triumphs.

4. Openness to Feedback and Adaptability

Green parents view feedback not as criticism but as a stepping stone to evolution and betterment. They instill in their children the value of continuous learning, emphasizing that feedback is a compass guiding growth. By actively seeking input and demonstrating receptivity in their own lives, they inspire their offspring to view feedback as a potent tool for self-refinement.

The ever-shifting dynamics of our world make adaptability a treasured attribute in the Green household. These parents mentor their children in the art of resilience and malleability, ensuring they possess the ability to recalibrate and adjust to evolving circumstances. This agility, they believe, not only allows their children to stay ahead of life's curveballs but also to thrive amidst them.

For Green parents, efficiency isn't just about saving time—it's about maximizing potential. They instill in their children the importance of strategic foresight and the judicious use of resources. By championing efficiency and effectiveness, they equip their children to leave impactful footprints in their endeavors.

Accountability is sacrosanct in the Green paradigm. Green parents nurture a culture of responsibility, guiding their children to be stewards of their choices. By owning up to decisions and their ripple effects, they believe their children gain robust self-awareness and an ingrained sense of self-determination.

Resourcefulness, in the Green parenting approach, is akin to empowerment. These parents foster ingenuity, urging their children to optimize available assets in surmounting challenges. Such a mindset not only nurtures innovative problem solving but also bolsters a child's confidence in their abilities to navigate hurdles.

Green parents emphasize the richness of diverse viewpoints. They mentor their children to be astute listeners and considerate thinkers, always seeking the broader picture before settling on decisions. Such an approach, they believe, not only yields well-rounded decisions but also broadens their children's horizons, gifting them a panoramic understanding of the intricate world they inhabit.

5. Emotional Stability and Objectivity

Green parents exhibit an unwavering emotional steadiness, acting as a pillar of strength and stability in their children's lives. They prioritize understanding over reprimand, grasping the essence that children are in an explorative phase of life, and errors are integral to the learning curve. By addressing misadventures with composure and logic, they ensure that children perceive mistakes not as failures, but as avenues of growth. This approach cultivates a secure environment where children are emboldened to introspect, learn, and progress.

Intelligence and rational thought are cardinal values in the Green parenting lexicon. While they exhibit patience, they do not mask their disdain for thoughtlessness or heedlessness. In instances of perceived incompetence, rather than resorting to unproductive rebukes, Green parents use these moments to underscore the significance of astuteness, diligence, and informed decision-making. The aim is not to belittle, but to elevate.

Embracing a quasi-scientific methodology, Green parents are akin to compassionate researchers. They keenly observe their progeny's behaviors and interactions, extract insights, and fine-tune their nurturing techniques to best align with their child's evolving persona. This empirical approach empowers them to offer bespoke care, tailored to resonate with each child's unique disposition and needs.

In a characteristic episode within a Green household, a young member returned, crestfallen after a school sports defeat. Instead of veering towards shallow comforts, the Green parent engaged their child in a reflective dialogue. They methodically navigated through the event, dissecting strengths and weaknesses, not as a critique, but as a collaborative analysis. The primary quest wasn't to dwell on the setback but to illuminate the road to future triumphs. As the conversation unfolded, the child's demeanor transformed—disappointment gradually metamorphosed into determination. This instance epitomized the Green parent's ethos: transmuting trials into constructive lessons, underpinned by emotional equilibrium and discerning objectivity.

However, this meticulous observation doesn't transmute into overbearing involvement. Green parents champion the philosophy of "present yet detached." They provide the necessary scaffolding but refrain from excessive interference, allowing their children the autonomy to blossom at their own pace, in their own space. Such trust in their offspring's capabilities fosters self-reliance and boosts self-esteem.

In the Green household, rules aren't arbitrary decrees but logical guidelines. Rather than inundating their children with a litany of do's and don'ts, these parents emphasize the underlying ethos that should guide actions and decisions. This not only promotes understanding but also equips children with the moral compass to navigate the intricate maze of life with integrity and wisdom.

6. Encouraging Self-Improvement

Green parents masterfully intertwine discipline with understanding. They operate on the tenet that discipline isn't about punitive measures but is rooted in enlightenment and guidance. Recognizing the inevitability of youthful transgressions, their focus remains steadfastly on rectifying the errant behavior rather than assigning blame. This nurtures a milieu where children comprehend the repercussions of their deeds without being mired in guilt or defensiveness.

The ability to decouple a child's essence from their actions is a hallmark of Green parenting. By refusing to label or stereotype based on isolated incidents, they ensure their children aren't boxed into restrictive and detrimental labels like "mischievous" or "clumsy". Their critiques are specific to actions, offering clarity on the unacceptability of a behavior and paving the way for introspection and amendment without damaging the child's self-worth.

On one particularly memorable occasion, a Green parent was approached by their child's teacher about a skirmish on the playground. Rather than reacting impulsively with reprimand, the parent chose to delve deeper into the situation. That evening, they sat down with their child, facilitating an open conversation about the incident. With gentle probing, it was revealed that the child had been responding to persistent teasing. Instead of simply admonishing the child for the conflict, the Green parent used this as an opportune moment to discuss alternative conflict resolution strategies. They explored ways to communicate displeasure, seek teacher intervention, and even brainstormed solutions to build better relationships with peers. The child emerged from the conversation not as a wrongdoer, but as an empowered individual equipped with better tools for interpersonal navigation.

Perpetual growth and relentless pursuit of excellence form the backbone of Green parents' philosophy. They envision high aspirations for their progeny, not as an oppressive burden but as an emblem of their faith in their child's potential. Far from leaving their children to grapple with these standards alone, they offer a reassuring presence, championing their victories and converting setbacks into lessons. This ethos fosters resilience, instills an indefatigable spirit of perseverance, and inculcates a mindset that views challenges as stepping stones to evolution.

7. Enjoying Intellectual Stimulation

Green parents are noted for their sharp wit and cerebral humor. Their jokes, rich in wordplay and references, might occasionally perplex the young minds in their company. While these intellectual jests might sometimes elude their children, they inadvertently seed a curiosity in them to delve deeper and embrace a nuanced sense of humor as they mature.

With a penchant for thoroughness, Green parents are akin to detectives when it comes to disagreements or dilemmas. Rather than succumbing to snap judgments, they meticulously gather facts, taking care to understand every facet of an issue. This methodical approach not only enhances the credibility of their decisions but also instills in their children the virtues of patience and informed decision-making.

The realm of parenting is ever evolving for Green parents. With a perpetual thirst for knowledge, they are in constant pursuit of innovative parenting techniques and discipline strategies. They are avid readers, workshop attendees, and are ever eager to glean insights from trusted experts. Yet, amidst this plethora of information, they possess the sagacity to sieve through and adapt strategies that resonate with their family ethos.

Surface-level conversations find little favor with Green parents. They gravitate towards profound dialogues that stimulate the intellect or shift paradigms. By delving into meaningful discussions with their offspring, they not only fortify their bond but also kindle in their children a penchant for introspection and a deeper understanding of their surroundings.

The idiosyncrasies of Green parents might occasionally lead their children to roll their eyes or blush with embarrassment. Be it a quirky hobby, an offbeat taste in music, or an unconventional fashion choice, their distinctive quirks stand out. However, as their children grow, they come to realize that these peculiarities are a testament to the beauty of individualism and an implicit lesson in embracing one's unique identity.

8. Promoting Responsibility and Problem Solving

For Green parents, a single set of instructions is considered sufficient. They operate under the belief that attentiveness is a vital skill and anticipate their children to be alert listeners. By not constantly reiterating themselves, they inadvertently nurture in their children a sense of responsibility, keen observation, and an aptitude to function without incessant supervision.

Choosing to omit the overtly evident, Green parents lay the groundwork for their children to cultivate analytical thinking. They steer clear of handholding, instead positioning themselves as guiding figures, offering direction without stifling independence. This philosophy sharpens the children's innate ability to decipher situations, fostering resilience and an analytical approach to challenges.

A defining trait of Green parents is their deep immersion in personal pursuits. Whether it's a hobby, research, or a pet project, their zest is palpable. While they maintain an unwavering commitment to their parental role, they also underline the importance of individuality and self-rejuvenation. Observing this, their children assimilate the essence of balancing personal passions with responsibilities.

Stimulating conversations are the hallmark of the Green parental style. They ardently champion intellectual exchanges with their offspring, touching upon diverse subjects and delving deep. Through these enriching conversations, children are not only emboldened to voice their perspectives but also acquire an insatiable curiosity and an appreciation for the vast expanse of knowledge that lies ahead.

9. Having a Strategic Approach

Green parents are synonymous with deliberate and methodical parenting. With a blueprint in hand, they set forth on their parenting journey, armed with well-defined objectives and outcomes in mind. This vision not only grants them the clarity to navigate parenthood with purpose but also allows them to impart consistency, ensuring their children enjoy a stable environment, irrespective of life's unpredictable turns.

Driven by a passion for honing their parenting acumen, Green parents covertly immerse themselves in a wealth of knowledge, ranging from parenting books to informative articles. While they avidly consume this information, they are discreet about their sources, choosing not to flaunt their continuous learning. This subtle approach underscores their intrinsic commitment to making informed choices and continually elevating their parenting techniques.

In a scenario reminiscent of this strategic approach, a Green parent was approached by their child with a request for a popular video game that "all the kids" were playing. Instead of giving an immediate yes or no answer, the parent took the time to research the game. They looked into its ratings, read reviews from both experts and parents, and even played a demo to understand its content and mechanics. They then sat down with their child and shared their findings, discussing the pros and cons of the game, its potential impact, and setting boundaries for playtime. The child, while initially eager for immediate gratification, grew to appreciate the reasoned approach and the mutual decision-making process that ensued. The experience not only resulted in a well-informed choice but also instilled a lesson about making deliberate decisions.

One would be hard-pressed to pull the wool over a Green parent's eyes. Renowned for their sharp discernment, they effortlessly see through facades and recognize ulterior motives. This skill transcends beyond their interpersonal interactions, playing a pivotal role in their parenting style. Leveraging this acumen, they mold their progeny into perceptive individuals, equipped with discerning minds and a prudent wariness of the world's complexities.

10. Valuing Knowledge and Understanding

At the core of Green parents' philosophy is the profound reverence for knowledge and understanding. They instill in their offspring an insatiable thirst for knowledge, viewing life as an unending educational journey. For them, classrooms are but one facet of education; real learning stems from a relentless quest for knowledge, driven by intrinsic curiosity.

Recognizing the monumental role the environment plays in nurturing intellect, Green parents ensure their homes reverberate with intellectual energy. These are homes where walls are lined with books, where debates are encouraged, and where inquisitive minds are met with answers and more questions. Their children are nurtured in atmospheres that not just feed their intellect but also challenge it, urging them to stretch their cognitive capacities.

In their pursuit of holistic education, Green parents underscore the significance of exploring myriad viewpoints. They advocate for the exploration of diverse narratives, driving home the lesson that truth often lies in nuances and shades of grey. This practice aids their children in breaking free from echo chambers, fostering a mindset that discerns, analyzes, and respects diverse viewpoints.

Ensuring that emotion doesn't cloud judgment is a cornerstone of the Green parent's ethos. While emotions are acknowledged and respected, they teach their children the invaluable skill of objective evaluation. Emphasizing the power of logical reasoning, they champion the cause of rational thinking, cultivating in their children the ability to make informed, objective decisions in a world teeming with biases and subjectivities.

Review

The journey with Green parents is one that carves individuals who are not just learned but also insightful, not just knowledgeable but discerning. With a robust foundation in rationality, an embrace of diverse perspectives, and an environment that challenges the intellect at every turn, children of Green parents are primed to become thought leaders of their generation. As they forge ahead, their paths illuminated by the wisdom imparted by their upbringing, they stand testament to the profound impact of the Green parenting paradigm—an approach that melds logic with love, understanding with guidance, ensuring a brighter, more enlightened future.

Green Parent Checklist

- ☐ Allow their children room to experiment and discover.
- ☐ Promote learning, not necessarily school.
- ☐ Aren't easily angered or upset by their children's actions.
- ☐ Have an overall parenting game plan.
- ☐ May read parenting books and magazines clandestinely.
- ☐ Won't be easily conned or hoodwinked.
- ☐ Become irritated at incompetence, foolishness.
- ☐ Believe raising children is like a lab experiment.
- ☐ Don't appear personally involved with their children.
- ☐ Won't hover, smother, and prod.
- ☐ Don't impose lots of unreasonable rules, limits.
- ☐ Promote self-directed decision-making.
- ☐ Teach principles that govern behavior, not detailed rules.
- ☐ Allow their children to experience natural consequences.
- ☐ Tend to question, cross-examine their children.
- ☐ Think through decisions before implementing them.
- ☐ Enjoy exploring new ways to parent, discipline.
- ☐ Avoid small talk with their children.
- ☐ Can embarrass their children with their peculiarities.
- ☐ Inspire their children to think outside the box.
- ☐ Tend to give instructions only once.
- ☐ Won't state obvious facts and insignificant details.
- ☐ Get caught up in their own projects.
- ☐ Enjoy intriguing, thought-provoking discussions.

- ☐ Administer discipline objectively, without prejudice.
- ☐ Easily separate behaviors from the person.
- ☐ Motivate their children to improve and progress.
- ☐ Often baffle their children with their puns, witticisms.
- ☐ Remain neutral while gathering facts.
- ☐ Foster curiosity and inquisitiveness in their children.
- ☐ Value intellectual development and critical thinking.
- ☐ Stimulate their children to question and challenge ideas.
- ☐ Equip their children with opportunities for intellectual growth.
- ☐ Are open to discussing complex topics with their children.
- ☐ Value logical reasoning and clear thinking.
- ☐ Uplift their children to seek knowledge and understanding.
- ☐ Provide a stimulating and intellectually challenging environment.
- ☐ Urge their children to not go along with the crowd.
- ☐ Value creativity and innovation.
- ☐ Train their children to solve problems on their own.
- ☐ Are open to new ideas and perspectives.
- ☐ Nudge their children to explore alternative theories.
- ☐ Value rationality and objectivity.
- ☐ Push their children to set and achieve intellectually challenging goals.
- ☐ Are open to constructive criticism and feedback.
- ☐ Guide their children to be adaptable and flexible.
- ☐ Value efficiency and effectiveness.
- ☐ Persuade their children to take ownership for their actions.

☐ Steer their children to solve problems with available resources.

☐ Encourage their children to seek out different perspectives before making decisions.

Chapter 6

The Orange Parenting Style

Embrace the world of Orange parenting and discover how to foster independence, positivity, and a love of life in your children. This guide will explore the key characteristics of Orange parenting, providing practical tips and insights to help you raise happy, confident, and resilient children. From promoting practicality and realism to encouraging flexibility and adaptability, learn how to parent the Orange way.

Orange Parent Summary

1. Boosting Independence and Freedom
2. Cultivating Positivity and Open-Mindedness
3. Supporting Physical Activity and Adventure
4. Fostering Social Interaction and Communication
5. Championing Practicality and Realism
6. Encouraging Flexibility and Adaptability
7. Instilling Confidence, Adventure, and Adaptability
8. Promoting Passion, Assertiveness, and Ownership
9. Living the Game of Learning
10. Embracing Life's Adventure of Choices and Challenges

Introduction

Parenting is a journey filled with its fair share of challenges and rewards. Each parent has their own unique style and approach that shapes the kind of environment they create for their children. For Orange parents, the focus is on fostering independence, promoting positivity and open-mindedness, and encouraging physical activity and adventure. This guide will dive deep into the world of Orange parenting, exploring the key characteristics that make this parenting style unique. From promoting practicality and realism to encouraging flexibility and adaptability, we will now reveal the top 10 things you need to know about parenting the Orange way.

1. Boosting Independence and Freedom

Orange parents believe in the power of self-determination and actively encourage their children to be independent decision-makers. They understand the importance of giving their children the freedom to explore the world on their own terms and to learn from their experiences. Instead of dictating every aspect of their children's lives, they provide guidance and support while allowing them the space to make their own choices and decisions. This approach helps their children develop a strong sense of self and the confidence to navigate the world on their own.

A key aspect of this philosophy is encouraging their children to have fun and enjoy life. Orange parents understand that life is meant to be lived to the fullest and they encourage their children to embrace every opportunity with enthusiasm and a positive attitude. They believe that having fun and enjoying life are essential components of a well-rounded and fulfilling life. Whether it's playing sports, creating art, or spending time with friends, Orange parents encourage their children to find joy in everything they do.

Another important principle for Orange parents is urging their children to "reach for the stars." They believe in the importance of setting ambitious goals and working hard to achieve them. They instill in their children the belief that with hard work, determination, and a positive attitude, they can achieve anything they set their minds to.

Orange parents also actively inspire their children to be adventurous and to take risks. They believe that stepping out of one's comfort zone and embracing new experiences is essential for personal growth and development. They encourage their children to try new things, meet new people, and explore new places. They believe that by taking risks and embracing the unknown, their children will develop a greater sense of self-confidence and resilience.

In addition to encouraging adventure and risk-taking, Orange parents also stimulate their children to be self-reliant and autonomous. They believe in the importance of teaching their children to take care of themselves and to be responsible for their own actions. They provide guidance and support, but ultimately encourage their children to take ownership of their lives and to make their own decisions. This approach helps their children develop a strong sense of self and the confidence to navigate the world on their own.

Orange parents promote proactivity and initiative-taking in their children. They believe that waiting for opportunities to come your way is not the most effective approach to life. Instead, they encourage their children to be proactive in seeking out opportunities and taking the initiative to make things happen. They believe that by being proactive and taking the initiative, their children will be better equipped to achieve their goals and to create a fulfilling and meaningful life for themselves.

2. Cultivating Positivity and Open-Mindedness

Orange parents are often described as good-natured and playful, with a youthful spirit that makes them seem more like kids at heart rather than strict authoritative figures. They approach parenting with a sense of humor and a light-hearted attitude, which helps create a positive and enjoyable environment for their children. They believe that a positive attitude is essential for a happy and fulfilling life, and they actively encourage their children to approach life with a sense of optimism and a focus on the positive aspects of any situation.

This positive approach to life extends to how they handle challenges and setbacks. Instead of dwelling on the negative aspects of a situation, Orange parents encourage their children to focus on the positive aspects and to approach challenges with a sense of confidence and determination. They believe that by focusing on the positive aspects of a situation, their children will be better equipped to overcome challenges and to achieve their goals.

In addition to promoting a positive attitude, Orange parents also actively discourage shyness, apprehension, and fear in their children. They believe that these emotions can be limiting and can prevent their children from fully embracing life and all it has to offer. Instead, they encourage their children to be confident, assertive, and outgoing. They believe that by fostering these traits in their children, they will be better equipped to navigate the world and to achieve their goals.

Orange parents are also known for being liberal, tolerant, and flexible in their approach to parenting. They believe in the importance of being open-minded and receptive to new ideas and experiences. They encourage their children to explore new activities, meet new people, and to approach life with a sense of curiosity and wonder. They believe that by being open-minded and receptive to new experiences, their children will develop a greater sense of self-awareness and a broader perspective on the world.

This open-minded approach to parenting extends to the home environment as well. Orange parents prefer a casual and laid-back environment at home, where their children feel comfortable and relaxed. They believe that a "free to be yourself" home environment is essential for their children's well being and development, which may mean they give children a long tether that allows them to grow and develop as they choose.

3. Supporting Physical Activity and Adventure

Orange parents are known for their active and adventurous lifestyle, and they actively promote physical activity and adventure in their children's lives. They believe that being active, athletic, and in good shape is essential for their children's physical and mental well-being. They encourage their children to participate in sports, outdoor activities, and other physical activities that promote fitness and health.

To make physical activity more enjoyable for their children, Orange parents often turn dull and mundane activities into entertaining games. For example, they might turn a simple walk in the park into a scavenger hunt or a race. They believe that by making physical activity fun and enjoyable, their children will be more motivated to participate and to stay active.

Physical play is also an important aspect of parenting for Orange parents. They often wrestle and play physically hard with their children, which helps promote physical strength and coordination. They believe that physical play is not only important for their children's physical development but also for their emotional and social development.

Orange parents often treat their children as pals and playmates rather than as subordinates. They believe that by treating their children as equals and by engaging in age-appropriate activities together, they can foster a strong bond and a sense of camaraderie. They often engage in activities that they enjoy as a family, such as hiking, biking, or playing sports.

This sense of adventure and love for physical activity extends to family outings and vacations as well. Orange parents will often drop everything to do something fun with the family, whether it's a spontaneous trip to the beach or a planned vacation to a new destination. They believe that by sharing these experiences with their children, they can foster a sense of adventure and a love for the outdoors.

Orange parents also often bring their children with them on their own adventures. Whether it's a hiking trip, a mountain biking adventure, or a rock climbing expedition, they believe that by exposing their children to new and exciting experiences, they can foster a sense of curiosity, adventure, and a love for the outdoors. They believe that these experiences are not only important for their children's physical development but also for their personal growth and development.

4. Fostering Social Interaction and Communication

Orange parents believe that social interaction and communication are crucial aspects of their children's development. They actively foster sociability and outgoingness in their children by encouraging them to interact with others, make new friends, and participate in group activities. They believe that by fostering these social skills from a young age, their children will develop strong interpersonal skills that will serve them well in the future.

Contrary to some parenting styles, Orange parents aren't opposed to arguing with their kids. They believe that healthy debate and discussion are important for their children's development and that it's important for their children to learn how to express their opinions, even if it means having a disagreement. They believe that by engaging in persuasive and passionate dialog, their children can develop critical thinking skills, learn to see things from different perspectives, and learn how to communicate effectively.

Humor is also an important aspect of parenting for Orange parents. They like to joke, tease, and play around with their children. They believe that humor is an important way to bond with their children and to create a positive and enjoyable environment at home. They also believe that humor is an important way for their children to learn about the world and to develop an optimistic outlook on life.

Orange parents also value play and recreation as important aspects of life. They believe that play is not only important for their children's physical development but also for their emotional and social development. They encourage their children to engage in play and recreation, whether it's playing sports, playing games, or engaging in competitive activities.

Orange parents inspire their children to be resourceful and independent. They believe that by fostering these traits from a young age, their children will develop the skills and confidence they need to navigate the world on their own. They encourage their children to be adaptable, to think creatively, and to find solutions to problems on their own. They believe that by doing so, their children will develop a strong sense of self-reliance and autonomy.

5. Championing Practicality and Realism

Orange parents understand that they live in a world dominated by Gold individuals, and that in order to succeed in life, you need to value the importance of structure, routines, and schedules, but they also acknowledge that they need help in providing these things. They recognize that creating a structured environment is important for their children's development, but they also understand their own limitations and seek help when necessary. They may enlist the help of Gold family members, friends, or professionals to create a structured and supportive environment for their children.

Orange parents also acknowledge that they aren't necessarily more responsible than their children. They understand that their children are capable of taking on responsibilities and making decisions on their own. They believe that by giving their children responsibilities and holding them accountable for their actions, they can foster a sense of responsibility and independence in their children.

While Orange parents tend to be overly generous and sometimes overindulge their children, they do so out of a desire to provide their children with the best possible life. They believe in giving their children the tools and resources they need to succeed and sometimes this means giving them more than they need. However, they also understand the importance of setting boundaries and teaching their children the value of hard work and perseverance.

Orange parents tend to complete household chores swiftly and resentfully. They prefer to spend their time engaging in activities that they find enjoyable and fulfilling rather than spending time on household chores. However, they also understand the importance of maintaining a clean and organized home and make an effort to complete chores as quickly and efficiently as possible.

Orange parents are pragmatic and focus on the here and now. They believe in taking action and getting things done rather than spending time worrying about the future or dwelling on the past. They encourage their children to focus on the present moment and to take proactive steps towards achieving their goals.

Orange parents are direct and straightforward in their communication. They believe in being honest and open with their children and encourage their children to do the same. They believe that by fostering open and honest communication, they can create a supportive and trusting environment for their children.

6. Encouraging Flexibility and Adaptability

Orange parents expect some degree of disobedience from their children, but they aren't dismayed by it. They understand that children are naturally excited about new things and may sometimes push the boundaries within themselves and others. Instead of getting upset or frustrated, they use these moments as opportunities to teach their children about the importance of respecting rules and boundaries while also encouraging them to be free agents and make their own decisions and accept the natural consequences.

Orange parents believe that when it's time to play, it's important to play with gusto. They encourage their children to fully engage in play and recreational activities and to enjoy themselves. They believe that play is an important aspect of a child's development and should be encouraged and supported. They believe everyone should spend at least some time each day involved in play.

While Orange parents aren't strict disciplinarians, they do believe in holding their children accountable for their actions. They may allow their children off the hook from time to time, but they also make sure to have conversations with their children about the consequences of their actions and the importance of making good decisions.

Orange parents are unpredictable and impulsive. They don't like doing the same things repeatedly. They enjoy variety and seek out new experiences and activities. They encourage their children to be open to trying new things and to approach life with a sense of fascination and wonder.

Orange parents get frustrated when their children don't "seize the day." They believe in making the most of each moment and encourage their children to do the same. They believe that by taking proactive steps towards hitting their targets and obtaining the prize, their children can lead fulfilling and successful lives.

Orange parents have a hard time sticking to schedules and timeframes. They prefer a more flexible approach to life and encourage their children to be adaptable and to go with the flow. They believe that by being flexible and adaptable, their children can better navigate the challenges and opportunities that life presents.

7. Instilling Confidence, Adventure, and Adaptability

Orange parents value spontaneity and living in the moment. They believe that life is unpredictable and it's important to be able to adapt to changing circumstances. They encourage their children to be spontaneous and to embrace the present moment. Whether it's an impromptu trip to the park or a spontaneous dance party in the living room, Orange parents believe that some of the best moments in life are unplanned.

They also urge their children to be adventurous and daring. They believe that taking risks and stepping out of one's comfort zone are essential for personal growth and development. They encourage their children to courageously take on new challenges, whether it's trying a new sport, making a new friend, or learning a new skill.

Orange parents motivate their children to be confident and assertive. They believe that confidence is key to success in all areas of life and they work to instill a sense of self-confidence in their children. They encourage their children to speak up for themselves, to express their opinions, and to stand up for what they believe in.

Oranges guide their children to be adaptable and flexible. In a world that is constantly changing, Orange parents believe it's important to be able to adapt to new situations and to be flexible in one's approach. They encourage their children to be open-minded and to be willing to change their perspective when necessary. They believe that by being adaptable and flexible, their children will be better equipped to navigate the challenges and opportunities that life presents.

8. Promoting Passion, Assertiveness, and Ownership

Orange parents equip their children with the tools to navigate life with both passion and pragmatism. While they understand the allure of dreams and aspirations, they also emphasize the significance of strategic planning and setting attainable goals. For every milestone reached, they celebrate with immediate rewards that are both meaningful and motivating. They instill in their children the importance of being of being passionate with everyday challenges, showcasing how a blend of realism and optimism can lead to success.

Assertiveness is a cornerstone in the teachings of Orange parents. Recognizing its importance in effective communication and self-advocacy, they motivate their children to voice their perspectives with confidence. This includes expressing their thoughts and emotions in a way that's both open and considerate of others. In doing so, they prepare their children to set boundaries, stand their ground, and articulate their desires in a world that's constantly evolving.

For Orange parents, life is an exhilarating journey meant for savoring. They instill in their children that the essence of life lies in its experiences, often emphasizing that moments lived with passion outweigh material possessions. They inspire their children to embrace every opportunity, be it exploring unfamiliar terrains, delving into novel activities, or forging new connections. It's this zest for life and exploration that Orange parents believe makes life truly fulfilling.

Ownership of one's actions is paramount in the Orange parenting playbook. They guide their children to recognize the power of accountability, viewing every setback as a steppingstone towards growth. Positive reinforcements, such as rewards that resonate with their child's desires, are used to amplify good behaviors. Just like immediate positive rewards reinforce positive behaviors (such as giving them something they want), immediate negative rewards (like taking away a treasured item or removing a valued privilege) corrects misbehaviors.

9. Living the Game of Learning

Orange parents get a kick when their kids try to pull a fast one on them. While some might scratch their heads, for Orange parents, it's like watching a live-action game of wit. They see it as their kids being clever, playing the game, and testing boundaries. Sure, they won't always let these sly moves slide, but they relish the challenge and turn it into a playful lesson on the art of straight talk.

For Orange parents, street smarts rival classroom lessons. They're fans of on-the-fly thinking and gut instincts. They coach their children to size up situations in real-time, trust their gut, and pivot when needed. It's not about what's in the books but how you play your cards in the real world.

They're the parents who'll give it to you straight, no frills. There's no dancing around the truth. They want their kids to see challenges as just another part of the game, knowing when to push forward or change tactics. It's about playing the game with both feet on the ground, knowing your strengths, and gearing up for the next round.

Every day is a new game level with Orange parents on the sidelines, cheering their kids on. Life isn't a drawn-out strategy; it's a series of exciting plays. They push their kids to dive in, take that shot, and savor every moment, be it a win or a lesson learned the fun way.

10. Embracing Life's Adventure of Choices and Challenges

Orange parents enjoy dynamic, in-the-moment exchanges with their kids. It's not about drawn-out debates but the thrill of spontaneous reactions and playful banter. They challenge their children to think on the spot, see different angles, and adapt swiftly. It's about prepping them for life's fast-paced game, where every move counts.

Discipline in an Orange household feels more like a strategy game. When rules are broken, it's not a one-way street. Kids are presented with choices: "Would you rather have no video games for a day or do an extra chore?" This approach turns discipline into a negotiation, making kids actively think about consequences and choose their path. It's less about punishment and more about understanding actions and their outcomes in a game-like setting.

Mistakes? They're just unexpected game twists for Orange parents. They recognize that life doesn't come with a manual and that kids learn best when they play, experiment, and occasionally land on a "Try Again" square. Their love isn't conditional on winning; it's about playing the game with heart and resilience.

Every day is a new game level for Orange parents. They motivate their kids to jump in, take risks, and chase the high score, whether that's personal growth, new skills, or simple joys. Every achievement, no matter its size, is a victory dance waiting to happen, and every setback is just a game restart, with new strategies to explore.

Review

Orange parents have a unique approach to parenting that focuses on fostering independence, promoting positivity and open-mindedness, and encouraging physical activity and adventure. They value spontaneity and living in the moment, and strive to instill these values in their children. By encouraging their children to be adventurous, confident, assertive, and adaptable, Orange parents are helping to raise the next generation of leaders, innovators, and troubleshooters. Remember, the goal is not to be a perfect parent, but to be a present one. Embrace the Orange within, and embark on this exciting journey of parenting with an open heart and an open mind.

Orange Parent Checklist

☐ Aren't bothered by being non-traditional parents.
☐ Promote being active, athletic, and in good shape.
☐ Like turning dull things into entertaining games.
☐ Expect disobedience and aren't dismayed by it.
☐ Promote freedom and self-determination.
☐ Are good-natured, playful, kids at heart.
☐ Allow their children to have fun and enjoy what life offers.
☐ Wrestle and play physically hard with their children.
☐ Treat their children as pals and playmates, someone to do things with.
☐ Urge their children to "reach for the stars."
☐ Share the limelight with their children; aren't behind the scenes.
☐ Need help in providing structure, routines, schedules.
☐ Believe when it's time to play, play with gusto.
☐ Aren't strict disciplinarians, allow their children off the hook.
☐ Will drop everything to do something fun with the family.
☐ Are unpredictable, impulsive parents.
☐ Aren't necessarily more parental than their children.
☐ Don't like doing the same things repeatedly.
☐ Enjoy watching their children try to con them.
☐ Get frustrated when their children don't "seize the day."
☐ Have a hard time sticking to schedules and timeframes.
☐ Tend to be overly generous and overindulge their children.

- ☐ Discourage shyness, apprehension, fear.
- ☐ Are liberal, tolerant, flexible parents.
- ☐ Aren't opposed to arguing with their kids.
- ☐ Bring their children with them on their adventures.
- ☐ Complete household chores swiftly, resentfully.
- ☐ Don't like to sit around the house and do nothing.
- ☐ Prefer a casual, laid-back environment at home.
- ☐ Like to joke, tease, and play around with their children.
- ☐ Inspire their children to take risks and be adventurous.
- ☐ Value spontaneity and living in the moment.
- ☐ Urge their children to be adventurous and daring.
- ☐ Are open-minded and receptive to new activities.
- ☐ Motivate their children to be confident and assertive.
- ☐ Value play and recreation as important aspects of life.
- ☐ Guide their children to be adaptable and flexible.
- ☐ Are optimistic and focus on the positive aspects of life.
- ☐ Foster sociability and outgoingness in their children.
- ☐ Value practicality and common sense.
- ☐ Inspire their children to be resourceful and independent.
- ☐ Are realistic and down-to-earth.
- ☐ Stimulate their children to be self-reliant and autonomous.
- ☐ Value action and getting things done.
- ☐ Promote proactivity and initiative-taking in their children.
- ☐ Are pragmatic and focused on the here and now.
- ☐ Train their children to be practical and realistic.
- ☐ Are direct and straightforward in their communication.

☐ Foster assertiveness in their children.
☐ Value experiences and living life to the fullest.

Chapter 7

How to Parent Aliens

In the vast universe of life, parenting often feels like making first contact with an alien, filled with moments of wonder, awe, and the occasional intergalactic miscommunication. Venture further into this chapter as we decode the intricate signals of our "alien" children, harmonizing our preferences with the unique frequencies of their personalities.

Venturing Beyond Our Parenting Comfort Zone

Imagine for a fleeting moment that you're gazing up at the vast expanse of the cosmos, each star and planet radiating its unique brilliance. Suddenly, an alien spaceship—vibrant and peculiar—descends, unlike anything you've seen before. This is akin to encountering a child whose personality type differs starkly from yours. Just as an astronaut must understand and adapt to the unfamiliar terrains of alien planets, so must we attune ourselves to our "alien" children.

Parenting is like watching the captivating dance of colors you might observe through the intricate lens of a kaleidoscope. Each color has its unique allure, but as they intermingle, a mesmerizing mosaic forms. In much the same tantalizing tapestry of hues, we all possess a distinctive parenting style—our personalized hue, if you will, in the vast spectrum of parenting approaches.

This is the very essence of our personal parenting style: a combination of experiences, values, and instincts that shape our interactions with our little ones. It's the invisible guidebook we unknowingly reference when deciding if a bedtime story warrants one more page or if that painting should indeed find a permanent spot on the living room wall.

Now, here's a quirky yet enlightening thought: What if parenting was like trying on hats? Imagine standing before a grand mirror, adorned in a hat that feels so quintessentially "you." It's comfortable, familiar, and fits just right. But, as you turn your gaze, you find an array of other hats beckoning. Some seem utterly ludicrous, others intriguing, but none quite as snug as your own. These represent the diverse parenting styles that differ from our own intrinsic methods. The real challenge? Mustering the audacity to try on a new hat and experience the world (or, in this case, parenting) from a fresh perspective.

Now, for most of us, the idea of venturing out of our comfort zones—especially in the delicate dance of parenting—might seem as daunting as attempting a tightrope walk on a windy day. Why fix what isn't broken? Why swap our trusty hat for an unfamiliar one? But, here lies the provocative thought that propels this chapter: In the adventurous journey of raising unique little humans, is it possible that our go-to, tried-and-true parenting style might not always be the best fit? Could there be merit in stretching beyond our comfort zones to better resonate with the individual temperaments of our children?

With a dash of humor, a sprinkle of compelling anecdotes, and a hearty dose of encouragement, let's embark on this introspective journey. We'll delve deep into the intricacies of our ingrained parenting styles, explore the boundaries we've consciously or unconsciously set, and dare to entertain the thought of occasionally donning a different hat. For in the vast world of parenting, sometimes it's the unexpected styles that lead to the most enriching and enlightening experiences.

The Trap of Parenting Through Personal Preferences

Consider, if you will, the story of Amelia, a classic Blue parent. Her heart overflowed with nurturing instincts, making her home a haven of warm hugs, bedtime stories that extended well past the designated page limits, and a pantry always stocked with homemade cookies. The aroma of freshly baked treats wafted through the air, signaling a sanctuary of love and understanding. Every scraped knee was met with a symphony of soothing words and gentle reassurances. For Amelia, her Blue parenting style, with its emphasis on emotional connection and understanding, was as intrinsic as breathing.

Then enters young Lucas, Amelia's Gold child. An embodiment of structure and routine, Lucas found solace in the predictable. His idea of comfort? A neatly arranged room, a well-structured day, and the subtle assurance of tomorrow's tasks clearly penciled into his planner—even if it just detailed his preferred playtime blocks. For Lucas, the impromptu cookie breaks and spontaneous story extensions were less "comforting surprises" and more "unexpected deviations." While Amelia believed she was offering layers of nurturing, Lucas often felt like he was being swaddled in an over-tightened blanket of spontaneity.

One day, when Amelia decided to transform their reading nook into a whimsical fort without prior notice, Lucas's exasperation peaked. "Mom, where's my reading light? And why is my book on the ceiling of the fort and not on the shelf where it belongs?" The fort, while a gesture of love from Amelia, became an emblem of disarray for Lucas.

This anecdote encapsulates a timeless trap many parents, even the most well-intentioned ones, often fall into: the pitfall of parenting purely through personal preferences. Amelia's heart was in the right place, but her approach—steeped heavily in her own Blue temperament—occasionally missed the mark with her Gold child.

When we, as parents, project our personal parenting style onto our children, the drawbacks are twofold. Firstly, we risk missing out on truly understanding and resonating with our child's unique needs. Not every gesture of love or discipline translates universally across temperaments. Secondly, our children, especially when still blossoming in their understanding of the world, might feel an unintended pressure to conform, to fit into a mold that doesn't quite align with their intrinsic nature.

In the grand tapestry of parenting, it's crucial to recognize that our natural inclinations, while valuable, might not always be the best fit for every child. It's akin to trying to complete a jigsaw puzzle using pieces from different sets. While they might seem similar, the nuances matter. In the quest to raise confident, well-adjusted children, it's paramount that we occasionally swap our trusty hats, striving to understand and cater to the diverse temperaments that our children present. For in the harmonious blending of our styles with their needs lies the true magic of parenting.

The Heartbeat of Harmonious Parenting

Imagine you're in a grand ballroom, where a mesmerizing dance is unfolding. Two partners, moving in sync, yet each possessing their distinct rhythm. This is much like the duet of parenting; the perpetual *pas de deux* between a parent and child. However, unlike a choreographed routine, parenting often comes without a script. It's an improvised dance, where success is predicated on one's ability to be attuned to the partner's steps. Enter the magnetic realm of Emotional Intelligence (EI).

Emotional Intelligence, often heralded as the lesser-celebrated cousin of IQ, is a luminary in its own right, particularly in the realm of parenting. It's the ability to perceive, evaluate, and respond to one's own emotions and those of others. Think of it as the compass guiding the ship of parenting, helping us navigate the sometimes turbulent waters of child-rearing. EI beckons parents to go beyond the surface, to dive deep into the unspoken feelings and sentiments, and to recognize that every tantrum or silent treatment has a backstory.

While our innate parenting style might advocate for a certain approach—be it a comforting hug, a stern word, or a logical explanation—Emotional Intelligence prompts us to pause, reflect, and choose a response that resonates with our child's emotional frequency at that moment. It's not just about "what" we do but understanding the "why" behind our child's behavior and tailoring our reaction accordingly.

But here's the provocative part: answering this call to EI requires us to embark on a journey of self-awareness and growth. It demands the maturity to sometimes sideline our innate responses, our personal comfort zones, in favor of what our child truly needs. Remember young Lucas and the whimsical fort? It's the maturity to recognize that while our Blue heart might wish to drown our child in affection, their Gold heart might be yearning for a touch of predictability.

It's not an easy feat, and therein lies the challenge. To continuously prioritize our child's needs over our instinctual responses requires an evolved sense of selflessness. But, in this altruistic act, there's an empowering realization: by cultivating our EI and understanding our child's unique temperament, we're not just becoming better parents; we're evolving as empathetic human beings.

The call to Emotional Intelligence is not a fleeting trend; it's a timeless anthem that has echoed through the annals of effective parenting. It's about setting aside the ego, embracing the echo of our child's feelings, and crafting responses that foster understanding and connection. As parents, our hearts might naturally dance to a certain beat, but by tuning into the symphony of our child's emotions, we can craft a harmonious melody that celebrates both our rhythms. And isn't that the ultimate goal? To create a harmonious household where every member feels seen, heard, and cherished.

Ah, but let's not be too hasty to think that mastering EI is the final destination. Far from it! Emotional Intelligence is akin to the ebb and flow of tides—dynamic, ever-changing, and responsive. As our children grow, traverse new terrains, and mold their identities, their emotional landscapes evolve, offering new horizons for us to explore. While today it might be about deciphering the unsaid emotions behind a scribbled drawing, tomorrow it could translate to reading between the lines of a teen's seemingly indifferent text message.

But this is where the magic lies. Armed with EI, parents are like seasoned sailors, skillfully adjusting their sails, ever-prepared for the changing winds. They become attuned listeners, who hear the whispers even amidst deafening silences. They morph into insightful observers, spotting the subtlest of nuances—a fleeting look of dismay, a momentary pause of hesitation, or the smallest quiver of the lip.

However, and let's be frank, sometimes the very act of prioritizing our child's needs over our personal preferences can feel like a Herculean task. There are days when our patience wanes thin, when the weight of responsibilities bears heavy, and our innate parenting tendencies scream to take the forefront. But here's the catch: It's on these very days, in these trying moments, that our commitment to EI shines brightest. For in our conscious decision to choose our child's emotional well-being over our momentary lapse, we send a powerful message. We tell our child, "You matter. Your feelings are valid. I am here for you."

Stepping into the realm of Emotional Intelligence doesn't entail relinquishing our parenting instincts altogether. Instead, it's about harmoniously marrying our natural inclinations with the acute awareness of our child's emotional needs. It's a delicate balance, a dance of finesse and grace.

Heeding the call of Emotional Intelligence is not merely a parenting strategy—it's a transformative journey. A journey that not only elevates our parenting prowess but also enriches our relationships, fortifying bonds with the unbreakable adhesive of empathy, understanding, and love. So, as we journey forth in the enchanting realm of parenting, let's let Emotional Intelligence be our guiding star, illuminating the path toward mutual respect, understanding, and a connection that stands the test of time.

From Self-Centered to Child-Centered Parenting

The winds of parenting often beckon us to embark on a journey, sailing away from the shores of our ingrained habits and docking our boats on the islands of self-awareness and understanding. But let's be honest—this journey is less of a smooth sail and more of a wild roller-coaster ride, rife with loop-de-loops of trial and error.

Take, for instance, the valiant effort of Mr. Park, a quintessential Gold parent. Armed with his prowess and affinity for detailed planning, he decided one day to inject a spontaneous burst of adventure into his household. Inspired by a book he'd recently read about catering to a child's temperament (the irony!), he deemed it fit to organize a spontaneous adventure day for his free-spirited Orange daughter, Ji-Yeon.

On the morning of this "spontaneous" outing, Mr. Park presented Ji-Yeon with a meticulously detailed itinerary, complete with time slots, activity lists, and emergency contacts. He'd even gone the extra mile to include color-coded charts for clarity! Ah, the hallmark of a Gold parent's love.

Little Ji-Yeon, with her vibrant Orange spirit, gazed at the document, her tiny brows furrowing in confusion. "Daddy," she began, hesitating, "Is this our adventure?" Mr. Park nodded enthusiastically, to which Ji-Yeon innocently retorted, "But... where's the adventure in knowing everything beforehand?"

And there, in that simplistic query, lay the profound wisdom of child-centered parenting. Ji-Yeon wasn't seeking a well-organized day out; she yearned for the thrill of unpredictability, the magic of the unknown, the zest of living in the moment—attributes intrinsic to her Orange temperament.

Recognizing our children's unique temperaments is akin to decoding the complex, intricate notes of a symphony. Each temperament—be it Blue, Gold, Green, or Orange—resonates with a distinctive rhythm, a beat that forms the very essence of their being. To harmonize with this rhythm, we must first attune our ears, stripping away the layers of our biases, and letting the pure, unadulterated notes of our child's temperament wash over us.

In our noble quest to be the best parents, we often forget a cardinal truth: Children are not mere extensions of our desires, nor are they blank canvases awaiting our master strokes. They arrive in our lives as unique, multifaceted individuals, each endowed with their own set of whims, fancies, and idiosyncrasies. It's our privileged task to recognize, respect, and revel in these individualities.

In hindsight, Mr. Park's humorous misadventure serves as a poignant reminder of this very principle. For in his well-intentioned yet misplaced effort, he uncovered a vital parenting gem: To truly connect with our children, we must journey beyond the realm of our personal preferences, venturing into the uncharted territories of their vibrant personalities.

As we tread this path, we'll need to figure out how to endure, and eventually cherish the stumbles and celebrate the discoveries. We need to make sure that our parenting compass always points towards the true north of our child's heart.

Journeying Beyond the "Me" to the "We"

There's an old adage that says, "Knowing oneself is the beginning of all wisdom." And while there's profound truth in these words, when it comes to parenting, there's a delightful twist: "Knowing oneself is only half the battle, embracing the nuances of our little ones completes the tale."

Imagine, if you will, the art of making a classic sandwich. Knowing your preference—whether you're a die-hard mayo enthusiast or a staunch mustard supporter—gives you a leg up. But what happens when you're making a sandwich for someone whose palate salivates to a different flavor profile? You've got two choices: slather on your favorite condiment and hope they'll learn to love it or, heaven forbid, ask them what they'd prefer. Such is the challenge of parenting in the realm of temperament.

Each of us, laden with our histories, experiences, and yes, our personality preferences, approach the world with a unique lens. This lens, often shaded by our dominant hue—be it Blue, Gold, Green, or Orange—colors our perceptions, judgments, and interactions. It's our default setting, the comfort zone we inherently drift towards. But herein lies the crux of our parenting challenge: our children don't always wear the same colored glasses.

Delving deep into the archives of parenting misadventures, let's consider Mrs. Kim, a Gold mother known for her penchant for structure and routine. Every morning, like clockwork, she'd present her young Green son, Min-Jae, with a neatly organized day planner, filled to the brim with schedules, lists, and to-dos. While her intentions were golden, Min-Jae often felt overwhelmed, yearning for the freedom to explore and ponder without time constraints. In Mrs. Kim's earnest attempt to provide structure, she inadvertently curtailed her son's natural Green tendencies for introspection and discovery.

Addressing our inherent biases and tendencies is much like navigating a ship through uncharted waters. While we might have a trusty map (our preferences) to guide us, the seas (our children's unique personalities) often have plans of their own. The waves might be choppy, the currents unpredictable, but it's our task to sail forth, adjusting our course based on the waters' whims, not merely our navigational comfort.

In the pageant of parenting, validating our children's distinct personality colors isn't just a gracious act—it's paramount. It's a declaration that says, "I see you, not as an extension of me, but as the splendid, multifaceted individual you are." It's an affirmation that their feelings, desires, and inclinations, no matter how different from our own, hold value.

To chart a successful parenting journey, we must remember that understanding our preferences, while crucial, is only the starting point. The real magic unfolds when we set sail beyond the confines of our comfort zones, venturing into the vast, vibrant oceans of our children's temperaments, armed with empathy, validation, and boundless love. Because, in the end, isn't that what parenting is all about? Embracing the dance of differences and cherishing the harmonies they create.

The Unveiling Canvas of a Child's Personality

Imagine a vast canvas, untouched and primed, eager for the artist's brush. This canvas mirrors the heart and mind of an infant—open, absorbing, and rich with limitless potential. As parents, we're often captivated, peering deep into those radiant baby eyes, pondering, "What tales will unfold across your life's canvas? Which hue will underpin your masterpiece?"

From the infectious giggles of infancy to the angst-filled declarations of adolescence, charting the evolution of a child's personality is an awe-inspiring voyage. In those formative years, it's all about absorbing impressions. Infants, with their enchanting coos, gurgles, and burps, and curious expressions, synchronize with the world, becoming immersed in every experience. For some, like the Blue baby, it could be an emotional outpouring upon hearing a melancholic tune, while for a Gold infant, it might be the peace found in predictable rhythms.

Transitioning from toddling steps to school strides, the canvas acquires depth and contrast. Friendships, challenges, and newfound interests introduce an array of tones. A Gold child might find solace in the methodical rhythm of school, while an Orange child's canvas bursts with dynamic strokes, each recess a new escapade.

Then, there's adolescence. A maelstrom of feelings, discoveries, urges, and awakenings. This phase is less about changing the core hue and more about exploring the diverse shades surrounding it. The Green teen might be lost in thought, pondering existential queries, while a Blue might pen profound musings in secret diaries.

A thought often flits through the minds of reflective parents: Can we foresee the dominant shades of our child's personality spectrum? It's as tempting as peeking into the future. However, while their foundational hue remains steadfast, the surrounding spectrum is fluid, influenced by genetics, environment, societal interactions, and those spontaneous, transformative moments that life spontaneously delivers.

Predicting the precise spectrum is much like foretelling the course a meandering stream might take through a valley. We can discern its source, predict potential turns, but its exact path? That remains the stream's mystery.

In life's vast gallery, our children's personalities don't just grow—they flourish, diversify, drawing from their core hue while incorporating the world's vast palette. As their first guides, our task isn't to dictate but to nurture. We offer understanding, love, and a sanctuary where they can blend their foundational color with myriad shades, crafting a portrait uniquely theirs.

In the finale, it's the unpredictability, the uncharted, and the journey of self-discovery that make each child's personality narrative so enchanting. Our privilege? To observe, aid, and be astounded by the emerging masterpiece.

Empowering Sprouts by Honoring Their Blooms

The art of parenting isn't just in raising our kids but in raising ourselves up a few notches to understand the kaleidoscope that is a child's mind. After all, isn't it a tad bit funny that we often forget we were once their age, brimming with hopes, dreams, fears, and endless questions about the universe (or why broccoli can't taste like chocolate)?

One paramount aspect of this self-elevation is diving deep into the sea of our children's preferences. By addressing their values, motives, and desires, we're not just being "good parents." We're becoming their allies, their cheerleaders, their guiding stars. But how do we go about this?

Strategy 1: Open Dialogue. The answers often lie in simple conversations. A nightly chat before bedtime, a discussion over breakfast, or even a heart-to-heart during a long drive can reveal much about what's brewing in their minds. Listen more, talk less, judge never.

Strategy 2: Observation Over Assumption. Watch their actions, their reactions, and interactions. Sometimes, a child's choice of toy, book, video game, or even a TV show can be a window into their intrinsic motivations and preferences.

Strategy 3: Encourage Exploration. It's alright if your Gold child wants to dive into arts for a while or if your Orange child takes a sudden liking to coding. Let them explore. It's through trials that they'll find their true calling.

Strategy 4: Create a Safe Space for Expression. Encourage your child to express their thoughts, feelings, and ideas without fear of judgment. Whether it's through art, writing, or simple conversation, letting them know that their voice matters can be a powerful tool for understanding their preferences and desires.

Strategy 5: Involve Them in Decision Making. Whether it's choosing the weekend activity or deciding on a family movie night pick, involve them in the decision-making process. This not only helps you discern their preferences but also reinforces their sense of autonomy and value.

Now, let's zoom in on a real-life tapestry—a case study that's as enlightening as it's endearing. Meet Jamie, a 7-year-old with a distinctly Green temperament. Jamie's world is one of logic, where every action has a reason and every question, no matter how baffling, demands an answer. His parents, initially, were flabbergasted by the recurrent tantrums. Why was asking him to wear his shoes such a drama? Or why did "eat your veggies" turn into a courtroom debate?

The turning point was when they decided to shift gears. Instead of the usual "Because I said so," they tried, "Let's figure this out together." When Jamie questioned why he needed to wear shoes outside, they discussed potential foot injuries and the discomfort of stepping on something sharp or icky. The logic appealed to Jamie's Green sensibilities. When veggies became the point of contention, they discussed nutrition, body growth, and even drew parallels to how plants need specific nutrients to grow tall and strong.

Tantrums transformed into teachable moments. Resistance turned into a quest for understanding. By catering to Jamie's logical leanings, his parents didn't just make their lives more peaceful but also enriched Jamie's learning experience.

As parents, it's essential to remember that each child sings their own unique tune. By acknowledging their preferences, we empower them. By understanding their world, we not only become a part of their journey but also let them become the heroes of their own beautiful, evolving stories.

The Delicate Dance of Parenthood

In the rhythm of parenting, there's a delicate dance. A two-step, a waltz, sometimes a frantic jitterbug, between our deep-seated desires as parents and the ever evolving needs and wants of our sprightly offspring. Parenting, as many of us realize rather quickly, isn't merely about shaping our children but also reshaping ourselves. And herein lies the question: How do we strike that perfect balance without tipping over and falling on your face?

Let's begin with a universally acknowledged truth: parenting is not an exact science. It's more of an art, really. One painted with strokes of compromise, shades of understanding, the vibrant colors of love and care, as well as some bold outlines that establish rules, boundaries, and limitations. But like every artist, a parent needs their own space, their own canvas, and their unique palette.

Step 1: Open Channels. Keeping an open channel of communication with your child is paramount. This isn't just about big life talks but about the daily nitty-gritty. Maybe you, a Gold parent, treasure structure and routines, but your little Orange cherub thrives on spontaneity. Discussing what each day might look like can create a blend of scheduled spontaneity. Monday might be meticulously planned, while Wednesday is a wild card!

Step 2: Personal Timeouts. Just as kids have their timeouts (sans the naughty corner connotations), parents too need their breaks. A Gold parent might treasure this time for meticulous planning, while a Green parent might spend it diving deep into thought. These pauses can recharge you and make interactions with your children more fruitful.

Step 3: Celebrate Differences. Instead of seeing differences as roadblocks, why not view them as opportunities? An Orange parent's adventurous streak can complement a Blue child's emotional depth. A camping trip, perhaps, where stories flow freely under a starry sky?

But here's a tantalizing thought to munch on: Can we ever truly set aside our parenting preferences? Dive into that mental pool for a moment. Preferences aren't just switches we can flick on and off. They're wired into our psyche, crafted by years of experiences, learnings, and, well, our very DNA.

Imagine a Gold mom, Clara. She's a stickler for schedules. Her day is a tight ship of tasks meticulously arranged in hourly slots. Then enters little Sam, her Green son, who can't understand why everything must be so "timey-wimey" (thanks, *Doctor Who*). One day, they struck a pact. Sam would respect three crucial schedules of the day—mealtime, study time, and bedtime. The rest? Well,

Clara allowed a little fluidity, much to her chagrin initially. But soon, she found herself enjoying the unpredictability, the joy of unplanned moments.

So, while we can't completely toss our preferences out the window, we can certainly adjust the blinds a bit. By understanding that it's not about changing our core but about flexing our approach, we can twirl, spin, and glide in this dance of parenting. Balancing our needs with our children's desires is not just a task but a journey, one where every step, misstep, and leap makes the dance even more beautiful.

Painting Tomorrow with Today's Palette

It's been said before (in fact several times in this chapter) that life is a canvas, and we are the artists. But when it comes to parenting, it's like creating a collaborative masterpiece with our little co-artists who have their own vision, albeit sometimes a tad kaleidoscopic and ever-changing. Our role? Sometimes, it's as simple—and as challenging—as handing them the brush and watching in awe as they color outside our carefully sketched lines.

Reflect back on the day you first held your little one. If you're anything like me, you probably had grand plans, and I mean grand. A vision of parenting perfection, curated from years of reading, wisdom from the ages, and, let's be honest, a few saved Pinterest boards. You, dear parent, were geared up with a style, a preference, a methodology. Then, along came your child, dancing to a tune that wasn't even on your playlist. And, amidst the cacophony of cuddles, cries, and countless lullabies, a new rhythm emerged.

However, as the initial years sprint by, laced with their own cocktail of joys, jolts, and jitters, the focus often subtly, almost imperceptibly, narrows down to "our parenting style." We become connoisseurs of our own ways, sometimes oblivious to the fact that our tiny humans aren't so tiny anymore. They're evolving, their personalities are taking shape, much like clouds on a breezy day—fluid, whimsical, and absolutely mesmerizing.

So, what's the grand takeaway here? Simple. Adjust the lens. Zoom out from the microscopic analysis of our parenting methodologies and focus on the magnificent mosaic of our children's personalities.

Let's paint an amusing picture, shall we? Imagine you, a steadfast Gold, have your week planned to a tee. And out of the blue, your eight-year-old Orange pops the question, "Why can't we have breakfast for dinner?" Now, before your Gold instincts kick in with a logical explanation on meal plans, take a pause. Delve deeper. Perhaps, behind that seemingly whimsical query lies a budding Orange's exploration into breaking norms and experimenting. Instead of brushing it off, entertain the idea, make it a fun "Opposite Day," and join in the excitement!

This journey of stepping back and letting their colors shine isn't just about them—it's equally about you. It's a symbiotic dance, one where understanding and adjustment are the keynotes. Your Blue child might weave tales where logic seems lost, but the emotional depth? Oh, it's the Pacific Ocean! Dive in with them, feel the ebb and flow of their tales, and appreciate the vibrant hues they bring into your world.

As we wade through the tumultuous yet thrilling terrain of parenting, let's shift our gaze forward and cherish the bigger picture. Embrace the spectrum, the colors, the nuances, and let's remember: every shade our children add makes the family portrait all the more splendid.

The Symphony of Flexibility

One last metaphor to drive this point home. Let's pretend you've painstakingly pieced together a thousand-piece jigsaw puzzle, each fragment holding a tale, a memory, a nuance. Now, at the verge of the final placement, you realize there's a piece that's, well, a smidgen misfit. What do you do? Force it in, hoping no one notices? Or step back, assess, and reconfigure?

Parenting is much like this puzzle. A beautiful, baffling blend of memories, methodologies, and occasional misadventures. But, in this rich tapestry of trials and triumphs, the real reward often isn't in the perfection of the pattern but in the adaptability of the approach.

Being adaptive in our parenting style is akin to being the conductor of an orchestra, where each musician (read: child) brings their own instrument and tune. While we might have our favorite melodies (yes, I'm looking at you, fellow Beethoven enthusiasts!), the magic truly unfolds when we appreciate the diverse instruments and allow each to play its part. It's not about suppressing the tuba so the violin can shine, but knowing when to let each have its solo moment.

And oh, the symphony that results from such adaptive conduct! The reward is an opus of understanding, a crescendo of connection, and a finale of familial harmony. It's watching your Blue child empathetically comforting their Gold sibling after a rough day, or observing the Green teen offer logical solutions to the Orange tot's imaginative escapades. It's about understanding that while we might be wired to enjoy a calm, serene waltz, our children might be all about that jazzy, jivey Charleston!

Now, while we're basking in the afterglow of these harmonious moments, let's peek into the looking glass of anticipation. If you thought this was a deep dive, brace yourself, for we're about to embark on an expedition into the Marianas Trench of understanding our children's personalities. Spoiler alert: It's deeper, darker, and will crush your bones to smithereens, but oh-so-enlightening!

As we turn the pages of this parenting playbook, the subsequent chapters promise a voyage like no other. We'll traverse through the meandering paths of personality development, decode the enigmas of emotional expressions, and most importantly, equip ourselves with the tools to not just understand but to truly connect with our young ones.

So, as we wrap up this chapter, remember: the realm of parenting is expansive, ever evolving, and eternally educative. While we might start our journey with a map etched in our preferences, the real treasures are discovered when we venture off the beaten path, led by the starry-eyed wonder of our children.

To adaptive adventures and beyond! Onward we journey, deeper into the heart and art of understanding our children's unique and vibrant personalities.

Chapter 8

Observing the Behaviors of Children: Ages 0-3

Dive deep into the mesmerizing realm of early childhood, unraveling the subtle cues and delightful displays of nascent personalities. This chapter illuminates the fascinating dance of temperament in infants and toddlers, guiding you through those pivotal first three years.

Understanding Personality from the Cradle to Adulthood

The complex journey of personality development, characterized by four primary types, starts much earlier than often recognized. From the early moments of infancy, the dominant personality type begins to manifest, forming the unique character and preferences of an individual. Remarkably, some attentive parents might sense the initial signs of these personality types even before their child is born—through the subtle kicks and movements in the womb or through impressions, intuition, or feelings they have about their unborn child.

Have you ever gazed into the eyes of a newborn and wondered what profound thoughts, dreams, and aspirations were dancing behind those baby blues? Okay, maybe they're primarily pondering milk or their next nap, but that doesn't mean there aren't inklings of a budding personality in there.

Meet our four dominant temperaments: the soulful Blue, the steadfast Gold, the analytical Green, and the spirited Orange. Before your little ones can articulate their worldviews or debate the virtues of mashed carrots versus pureed peas, they give us glimpses into which of these temperament categories they might lean towards. It's like nature's little spoiler alert, if you will.

Picture this: Little Alex, barely six months old, has a penchant for gazing deep into your eyes, seemingly probing your very soul. It's as if he's silently whispering, "I feel you." There's an emotional depth and connection that's quintessentially Blue. And then there's Jamie, who, despite her tender age, already seems to have a schedule she's rather committed to. Interrupt her nap time and face the (adorable) wrath of a budding Gold.

You might chuckle thinking it's merely chance, but studies have suggested babies as young as three months can exhibit traits pointing to their future temperament. That's right! Before they can crawl, they're already giving us a sneak peek into their personality playbook. For instance, some infants might showcase a Green streak by being particularly inquisitive, turning their heads at the drop of a pin or the tick of a clock. They're the budding scientists, after all, forever questioning the world around them. Not to be outdone, the Orange babies might give you a run for your money, displaying their dynamic energy, probably making you wonder if there's an infant-sized marathon they're secretly training for.

And here's a compelling nugget of knowledge for you: our genes play a stellar role in shaping these temperaments. You might have heard someone say, "Oh, he's got his mother's eyes." But what about, "He's got his father's analytical mind"? Yes, genetics play their part, not just in determining eye color, but in influencing temperament too.

Recognizing and understanding these temperaments isn't just a delightful parlor game—it's the first step in nurturing and guiding our young ones in a manner that resonates with their core being. So, the next time baby Mia throws a fit when her toy is misplaced, remember, she might just be a Gold in the making, already valuing order and consistency.

Our journey with temperaments is akin to reading an enchanting novel, filled with plot twists and riveting characters. So, buckle up, because whether you're a parent, guardian, educator, or just an intrigued bystander, you're in for a treat as we dive deep into the fascinating world of infant temperaments, one adorable trait at a time.

Genetics, Environment, and the Dance of Personalities

Nature versus nurture—an age-old debate that's seen more rounds than a heavyweight boxing championship. But when it comes to temperament in infancy, it's less of a battle and more of a harmonious ballet, where genetics and environment pirouette gracefully around each other. Let's delve into this captivating choreography and see how our four temperaments take center stage.

Every infant is born with a genetic code, a kind of biological sheet music if you will. It's fascinating to think that right from the get-go, they might have genetic predispositions that hint at whether they'll be a reflective Blue or an ever-curious Green. Studies have unveiled patterns where certain temperamental traits, such as sensitivity or assertiveness, can often be traced back through family trees. Remember Aunt Lydia's passionate spirit? You might just see shades of that in your little one, hinting at a vibrant Orange temperament.

While genetics sets the stage, environment plays its tune, shaping and influencing how these temperaments manifest. The early environment—from the lullabies sung to the first books read—can either amplify or modulate these inherent traits. A Gold baby might thrive in a consistent routine, while an Orange might blossom when exposed to varied stimuli. It's a perpetual dance, with genetics providing the steps and environment leading the flow.

From as early as a few months old, babies can surprise you with bursts of temperament that align with our four categories. A Blue infant might be more responsive to facial expressions, mirroring emotions and showcasing an early empathy. In contrast, a Gold might find comfort in predictability, showcasing distress if their beloved teddy bear isn't in its "rightful" place at bedtime.

Ever witnessed an eight-month-old tirelessly figuring out how a toy works, not giving up until they've cracked its mechanism? You might be looking at a budding Green, showcasing early analytical prowess. And for those babies who seem to be in perpetual motion, exploring every nook and cranny with boundless energy? They're giving us a delightful preview of the dynamic Orange spirit.

When gazing at an infant, it's awe-inspiring to think of the whirlwind of factors at play, shaping their budding personalities. As genetics strums the chords, environment plays the melody, together composing the unique symphony of temperament for each child. Recognizing these early signs allows us to foster an environment tailored to each child's essence, setting the stage for them to dance confidently into their future.

The Developmental Milestones: Where Personality Meets Playfulness

As we delve into the developmental milestones of early childhood, it's crucial to understand that these stages might send out what we can call "false positives" in temperament identification. Each child, regardless of their inherent personality, will typically experience stages that seem to exhibit characteristics of Blue, Gold, Green, or Orange temperaments. However, these behaviors are a natural part of growth and not necessarily indicative of a child's core temperament. It's only when a child shows a consistent preference for certain behaviors or seems to resonate deeply with a particular stage that we might begin to see the true colors of their personality blossoming.

Somewhere around two months, a ray of sunlight pierces through babyhood—the social smile. Far more than mere reflexes or (sorry to burst the bubble) just gas, this may be a Blue in the making! This genuine grin, shared with caregivers, is an early sign of the deep connections and warmth that characterize the Blue temperament. As they seem to say, "Hello world, I'm open-hearted!"

Zoom to about 8 months, and a critical realization dawns: the world is full of mysteries waiting to be understood! The discovery of object permanence—that toys don't vanish when out of sight—could be a pure Green trait. Much like the adult Greens who relish theoretical complexities, these little ones are starting their quest for understanding the world's mechanisms, one hidden toy at a time.

Then comes the poignant moment between the end of the first year and the onset of the second: the adorable clinginess and the tears when parting from a primary caregiver. This isn't mere baby melodrama but perhaps a young Gold's foundational exploration of trust and attachment. Valuing security and commitment, Golds in the making are gauging their safe havens in the vast world.

Aha, here's where the Orange zest bursts forth! As our little adventurers start to roll, crawl, or take their first wobbly steps, the Orange temperament shines. Every inch of space is a new frontier, and each toy (or household object) a tactile treasure. This unbridled enthusiasm and hands-on exploration are early indications of the dynamic, spontaneous, and fun-loving nature of the Orange personality. Whether it's the thrill of toppling a tower of blocks or the impish delight in a game of chase, these little Orange explorers are all about living in the vibrant present.

From first smiles to first steps, every action of an infant is a page in the delightful diary of temperament discovery. Blues lay emotional cornerstones, Greens spark their cognitive curiosities, Golds build trust bridges, and Oranges? They're already hosting the party of life! As caretakers, our task is not just to witness but to appreciate, understand, and nurture these emerging hues of personality. Cheers to the grand symphony of babyhood, where every coo and crawl sings a note of nature's design!

The Blue Baby Chronicles: When Empathy Begins in the Bassinet

Swaddle up for a tale most tender. Here, in the comforting confines of the crib, amidst the lullabies and lingering dreams, we might just catch the earliest whispers of the Blue temperament. Before words, before steps, and certainly before they pen their first philosophical poem on the meaning of mashed peas, these infants showcase an ethereal essence, signaling the empathetic souls they're set to become.

Even before they can crawl, Blue babies exhibit exquisite emotional radar. When mommy's brow furrows or daddy's voice quivers, they respond. A lowered lip, a puzzled pout—it's as if they're absorbing the ambient feelings. Their reactions to emotional stimuli are akin to a finely tuned harp resonating with the room's emotional notes. You won't see them riveted by the latest cartoon; instead, these young souls exhibit a marked preference for human faces. To them, every wrinkle, every eye-twitch, is a tale worth attending to. A grimace from a sibling, a chuckle from grandpa, and our Blue baby is all eyes and ears, often mirroring those very emotions.

Now, let's talk attachment. While every baby forms bonds, Blue babies seem to seek something deeper. Their bonds feel less like chains of dependency and more like ancient, ethereal connections. It's as if they're saying, "I don't just need you; I feel you." In their eyes, you might just catch the glimmers of old souls searching for kinship and understanding, even in this tender phase of infancy.

Ah, the playground of the Blue baby! It's here that the role of imaginative play takes the center stage. While other tots might be content playing peek-a-boo, our Blue wonders might just be imagining a whole story behind it. "Why does teddy bear disappear? Where does he go? Is he on a grand adventure?" Their play isn't merely tactile; it's deeply imaginative. The smallest toys become protagonists in epic tales of valor, love, and idealism.

Before the age of realism sets in, our Blue infants showcase an early penchant for idealism. While they might not voice it out, their choices often lean towards harmony. The way they might offer their favorite toy to a crying peer or pat the back of a stuffed animal mimics the nurturing nature they'll come to epitomize.

To witness a Blue baby is to see the nascent stages of a compassionate, empathetic, and deeply feeling individual. From their early reactions to emotions to their budding idealism in play, they beckon a future where feelings and relationships reign supreme. So, the next time you see an infant entranced by human emotions or crafting imaginative tales in the sandbox, remember, you might just be in the illustrious company of a budding Blue soul. An encouraging thought, isn't it?

How to Spot a Blue Infant and Toddler

Deep Emotional Connections. From their very first coos and cries, Blue babies exhibit an innate capacity for emotional resonance. When a parent feels joy, they giggle in kind, and when there's sadness in the air, they seem to intuitively tune into that melancholy. It's as if their tiny hearts are already pulsing with an empathetic rhythm, syncing seamlessly with the emotional ebb and flow of their environment.

Intuitive Interactions. Even before they can articulate words, Blue infants have a unique way of communicating through soulful gazes and affectionate gestures. Their eyes often search for faces, seemingly trying to read the emotions and intentions behind every smile or frown, making connections on a profound, intuitive level.

Early Signs of Idealism. While their understanding of the world is still budding, Blue toddlers showcase a budding idealism. They might exhibit distress at the sight of another child crying or show an early preference for stories that end in harmony and happiness. There's an innate desire to see and make things right in their tiny universe.

Attachment and Depth. While all infants form attachments, Blue children tend to form deep bonds with caregivers, siblings, and even certain toys. These bonds aren't superficial; they seem to be rooted in a genuine desire for understanding and emotional depth. It's not just about being held; it's about feeling truly connected.

Imaginative Play. The playground of a Blue toddler is filled with vivid narratives and dreamy scenarios. A simple tea party becomes a grand gathering of fantastical friends, and bedtime stories come alive with their imaginative input. Their play isn't just play; it's a rich tapestry of tales and emotions.

Sensitivity to Stimuli. The world is a symphony of sensations for the Blue child. They might be more sensitive to loud noises, bright lights, or even the texture of their baby clothes. This sensitivity isn't just physical but extends to emotional stimuli, making them more attuned to the feelings and needs of others.

Desire for Harmony. Even in their early years, Blue children seem to have a penchant for peace. They might try to appease a fellow toddler who's upset or has become particularly unsettled in discordant environments. Their little souls yearn for equilibrium and emotional harmony.

Empathetic Mimicry. Blue toddlers often mirror the emotions and actions of those around them. If a parent is dancing, they'll jiggle along; if a sibling is upset, they'll offer a comforting toy. This mimicry is an early indication of their empathetic nature, always trying to connect and comfort.

Rich Emotional Expressions. A Blue child's face is a canvas of emotions. From the radiant joy of discovering a new toy to the profound sorrow of a scraped knee, they don't hold back in expressing their feelings. Their emotional palette is vast, and they paint with broad, genuine strokes.

Curiosity About Emotions. While many toddlers are curious about the world around them, Blue children are especially intrigued by the world within. They're the ones who'll point at tears, puzzled, or hug a friend spontaneously. Their questions, even if not verbalized, often revolve around the why's of feelings, hinting at the deep thinkers they're set to become.

Tiny Tidbits of Traditions: Spotting the Glittering Gold in Younglings

Once upon a sunlit morning, in a room that's meticulously ordered with teddies seated just so and toy trains arranged in an exact sequence, a story unfolds. It's the chronicle of the Gold child, a tale of tradition, tenacity, and teeny-tiny tokens of trustworthiness. Join me, as we embark on this scintillating sojourn, discovering the dawning days of our diligent Gold darlings.

Remember the bedtime story that's asked for every night? The same one? Over and over? Ah, yes. That's the work of our Gold child. There's a delightful dance in their dedication to routine. While other toddlers might hanker for novelty, our Gold gems thrive on the familiar. Their comfort? Patterns. Their joy? Predictability. From the precise angle they like their sandwich cut to the particular lullaby they insist on hearing, Gold children's emphasis on routines and patterns is palpable. The comfort of consistency cannot be overstated for these little souls.

To appreciate the importance of routine for a Gold child, one only has to witness the day their favorite toy goes missing or when their beloved bedtime storybook is swapped out. The reaction? It's akin to a fisherman realizing he's forgotten his fishing rod on the day of a big catch. It's not mere annoyance; it's a genuine disconcertment. Gold kids aren't just creatures of habit; they're its champions. When the familiar patterns they adore are disrupted, their reactions can range from mild irritation to deep-seated discomfort.

Ever seen a toddler meticulously placing their toys back in the toy box after play? Or perhaps you've noticed a little one "feeding" their stuffed bear, ensuring Mr. Teddy isn't left hungry? These aren't random acts; they're the earliest embers of responsibility igniting within our Gold children. Their toys aren't just playthings; they're charges under their conscientious care. A Gold child might mimic caregiving behaviors they see, embodying a precocious sense of duty. They're the youngsters you can trust to not color outside the lines, and if they ever did, they'd probably apologize to the paper.

In the heartwarming habits of the Gold child, we get glimpses of the responsible, reliable, and remarkably steadfast adults they're set to become. Their emphasis on order, their dedication to duty, even in the realm of rattles and race cars, is a testament to the age-old adage: old souls can indeed reside in young bodies. As we watch them flourish, we can't help but anticipate the remarkable resonance of responsibility and routine they're bound to bring into the world. Here's to the Gold children, tiny torchbearers of tradition in the tapestry of toddlerhood!

How to Spot a Gold Infant and Toddler

Creatures of Comfort and Consistency. From their earliest days, Gold infants display a penchant for predictability. The familiar lullaby, the same bedtime routine, the cherished cuddly toy—these constants provide a sense of security. Disruptions to their schedule, like a delayed mealtime or an unexpected outing, might be met with notable distress, signaling their inherent desire for structure.

Mimicry of Responsibility. Even before they can walk, Gold toddlers seem keen on emulating responsibility. You might find them trying to "clean" by wiping surfaces with a cloth or imitating parents by "cooking" in their play kitchen. These early actions are not just acts of imitation but the initial stirrings of their responsible and orderly nature.

Keen Observers. Gold children are often exceptionally attentive, taking in their surroundings with earnest eyes. They're the babies who notice if their favorite toy has been moved or if a regular visitor is missing from the family gathering. This observational acumen is part and parcel of their structured and detail-oriented mindset.

Early Respect for Rules. Even in their tender years, Gold toddlers exhibit a respect for boundaries. They are the ones who might hesitate before touching a forbidden object or look to their caregivers for approval before venturing into a new play activity. This early inclination highlights their intrinsic value for order and propriety.

Attachment to Tradition. Though still forming their understanding of time and events, Gold children often show a budding appreciation for traditions. They relish the repetitive reading of a cherished bedtime story or the recurrent play of a particular game, finding comfort in these familiar rituals.

Sensitivity to Social Order. In a playgroup setting, the Gold toddler might be the one who is wary of the boisterous kid or who tries to ensure that everyone gets a turn with the toy. They exhibit early signs of social consciousness, an inclination to maintain a sense of order and fairness in their interactions.

Pride in Accomplishments. Gold children, even at this age, exude a palpable pride in their achievements. Be it stacking blocks, completing a simple puzzle, or helping with a household chore, once accomplished, they often look to their caregivers for recognition, their faces beaming with the joy of achievement.

Caution in Exploration. While curiosity is a hallmark of childhood, Gold infants and toddlers approach exploration with a touch of caution. They're not the first to jump into a messy play or climb a daunting playground structure. Instead, they assess, take their time, and venture forth once they feel a sense of security.

A Loyal Little Buddy. Loyalty begins young for Gold children. They often have that one toy or blanket they're particularly attached to, symbolizing their budding trait of loyalty. This steadfastness, even in their choice of comfort objects, is a glimpse into the reliable and faithful individuals they're blossoming into.

Response to Positive Reinforcement. Gold toddlers thrive on positive reinforcement. A word of praise, a nod of approval, or a simple thumbs-up can light up their world. They're eager to please and find genuine satisfaction in knowing they've met expectations, laying the foundation for their future roles as dependable and diligent individuals.

Little Logicians: Glimpsing the Glint of Green in Gurgling Infants

Picture, if you will, a pristine playroom, painted in pastels, populated with plushies, and punctuated with the periodic giggles of giddy toddlers. Amid this delightful din, there's little Leo, not just poking at his puzzle but pondering its properties. While others are entranced by the twinkling toys, Leo's lit with a luminescence of a different sort. He's not just playing; he's probing. Welcome to the wondrous world of our Green-tinged tots, where every rattle is a riddle and every bauble, a brainteaser.

From the moment the morning rays meander into the nursery, the Green gem is on a quest, a mission of monumental magnitude. That mobile twirling above the crib? It's not just a toy. For our Green guppy, it's a tantalizing trajectory puzzle, a dance of dynamics and dimensions. Their curiosity isn't casual; it's critical. As they crawl and cruise, they're not just traversing the tiles but tackling the topography of their tiny territories. From the echo of their own babble to the shadow of their sippy cup, everything is an enigma awaiting elucidation.

Step into the sanctuary of a Green sprout, and you might marvel at their meticulous selection of playthings. Forget the fanciful fluff; their favorites are the toys that tickle the thinking. Building blocks that beckon balance, shape sorters that suggest symmetry, and even musical instruments that introduce intervals and tones. It's not about mere merriment; it's about mind-building mirth. For these diminutive dynamos, playtime is prime time for cognitive cultivation.

Introduce a puzzle, a challenge, perhaps a perplexing picture book, and watch the Green's gears grind with gusto. Where others might meander or mope at the monumental, our Green gazer gazes, gears up, and gets going. Novel stimuli? They don't daunt but delight. Whether it's a new nesting toy or a tricky tactile teaser, the reaction is rarely resignation but always resolution. There's a palpable passion in their pursuit, a clear craving for comprehension.

As we traverse the terrain of tots, the Green glimmers guide us to a unique utopia. A land less about lullabies and more about logic, less about rote and more about reasoning. As caregivers, educators, or enamored onlookers, our endeavor is not just to entertain these earnest explorers but to empower their endless expeditions. For in their questions, in their quests, lies the quantum leap of our collective cognition.

So, the next time you spot a sprightly sprite scrutinizing their surroundings or dissecting a toy's dynamics, tip your hat. You're in the illustrious presence of a Green-in-the-making, the future philosopher, the budding brainiac of our beautiful biosphere. And isn't that a gratifying glimpse into the grandeur of growth?

How to Spot a Green Infant and Toddler

Unquenchable Curiosity. From the cradle, Green infants exhibit an insatiable thirst for understanding. They're the babies who, instead of simply playing with a toy, will inspect it, perhaps even attempting to discern how it works. Their bright eyes seem to ask "why" and "how" long before they can articulate these questions verbally.

Problem-Solving Prodigies. Even in their infantile stages, Green toddlers display an innate knack for problem-solving. Whether it's figuring out how to retrieve a toy just out of reach or deciphering the mechanics of a new gadget in their crib, their analytical abilities shine bright, revealing their budding critical-thinking prowess.

Intense Focus. Green children, even amidst the distractions of toddlerhood, can exhibit remarkable bouts of concentration. They might spend extended periods engrossed in a single activity, be it stacking blocks in precise patterns or observing the wheels of their toy car turn, showcasing an early penchant for deep focus.

Fascination with Patterns. Patterns, sequences, and order—these are the realms where our Green infants thrive. They might show a preference for toys that allow pattern recognition or sequencing, like arranging rings on a peg in size order or grouping toys by color, reflecting their logical and structured mindset.

Early Independence. Even before they hit their "terrible twos," Green toddlers often show signs of valuing their independence. They might resist assistance, wanting to figure things out on their own, revealing an intrinsic drive to rely on their abilities and understanding.

Attraction to Novelty. New stimuli? Bring it on! Green children often gravitate towards the novel and unfamiliar. A new toy or a unique sound can captivate their attention, not just because it's different, but because it presents a fresh puzzle for their agile minds to decipher.

Precocious Communication. Though all children develop at their unique pace, Green toddlers might showcase early linguistic prowess. Their vocabulary, sentence structure, or the complexity of their questions can sometimes leave adults amazed, if not a tad overwhelmed by their precociousness.

A Rational Approach to Emotions. While every toddler has their moments of emotional meltdown, Greens often exhibit an interesting balance. They might try to understand their feelings or the reasons behind their discomfort, showcasing an early inclination to process emotions with a touch of logic.

A Keen Observer. The world is a vast laboratory for our Green infants. They often prefer to sit back and observe before diving into a new activity. Watching others, understanding the rules of a game, or simply contemplating the cause and effect in their environment, they're collecting data for their mental repositories.

Persistence in Exploration. When a Green child is on a mission to understand or master something, their tenacity knows no bounds. They'll attempt tasks repeatedly, tweaking their approach each time until they achieve their goal. This early perseverance is a testament to the analytical, driven individuals they're on the path to becoming.

Tiny Trailblazers: The Oranges in the Orchard of Infancy

Nestled amid the comforting cocoon of nursery nooks, where lullabies linger and pacifiers pacify, there's a bubbling brew of boundless energy. A whirlwind of wriggles, a dynamo of dauntless daring. Welcome, dear reader, to the realm of our Orange offspring, where every moment is a magnet for movement, and life is a luminous landscape of lively leaps and lunges.

Imagine this: Little Olivia, barely a year old, is not just content with crawling. No siree! She's on a mission, beelining for the balcony, scaling the sofa, and treating every cushion as her personal trampoline. Where other infants might be content examining their toes, our Orange Olivia sees them as tools for her next titanic task. Her heightened physical activity is not mere motion—it's a manifestation of her innate need for sensory engagement and exploration. The world isn't just a place to be—it's a playground to be pounced upon.

Introduce a new physical challenge and watch the Orange's eyes light up like a Christmas tree. Remember the day you brought home that mini slide? While others hesitated, our audacious Alex was already at the top, ready to slide down with a gleeful giggle. For him, challenges aren't roadblocks; they're roller coasters. Whether it's climbing a set of stairs, chasing a rolling ball, or waddling through water puddles, the Orange infant greets every challenge with a chirpy cheerfulness.

Ever noticed how some toddlers take a tumble and then, with a grin and a shrug, get right back up as if gravity was just playing a friendly game? That's our Orange Oscar for you! With an adaptability that'd put chameleons to shame, these tots have a go-with-the-flow gusto that's genuinely awe-inspiring. A sudden change in plans, a surprise visit to the vet (because teddy caught a cold), or an impromptu dance in the rain—to the Orange infant, it's all a part of the grand adventure of growing up.

As the tapestry of toddlerhood unfolds, amidst the tranquil Blues, the reliable Golds, and the analytical Greens, the Oranges stand out, not just in hue but in heart. They remind us of the sheer joy of living in the moment, of the thrill of the chase (even if it's just chasing after a butterfly), and of the beauty of bouncing back. Here's to our Orange infants and toddlers, the zestful zenith of zeal, teaching us that sometimes, life's greatest adventures are found in its smallest moments. Cheers to the champions of change, the titans of today, and the wonders of the "what's next"!

How to Spot an Orange Infant and Toddler

Born Adventurers. From the moment they muster the strength to crawl, Orange infants seem to have an innate wanderlust. They're the daring explorers of the nursery, venturing into every nook, cranny, and toy box. Their boundless curiosity ensures they're always on the move, chasing after new sights and sounds.

Sensory Mavericks. Taste, touch, sight, sound, and smell—each is a playground for our Orange toddlers. They might be found savoring the textures of their food, reveling in the squishiness of mud, or dancing joyously to the rhythm of their favorite tunes. Their world is a sensory fiesta, and they are its most jubilant attendees.

Instant Gratification Seekers. When an Orange child wants something, they want it now. Whether it's a toy, attention, or a snack, they're driven by the desire for immediate fulfillment. This spontaneity is a testament to their live-in-the-moment ethos, even in their diaper-clad days.

Social Butterflies. Even before they master their first words, Orange infants often display a magnetic charm. They're the little ones who'll flash a cheeky grin at strangers, initiate play with peers, or captivate a room with their bubbly energy. Their social prowess ensures they're seldom alone in the playground.

Physical Prodigies. Whether it's scaling the sofa long before they walk or showcasing impressive dance moves to a jingle, Orange toddlers often exhibit advanced physical capabilities. Their love for movement, coupled with their fearless approach, makes them agile and coordinated explorers.

Adaptable and Resilient. Change of plans? No problem! Orange children tend to take life's little detours in stride. They adapt to new situations with an ease that can often surprise adults. If their toy breaks or a playmate takes a cherished item, they might simply move on to the next adventure without much fuss.

Playful Pranksters. A mischievous sparkle in their eyes and a penchant for playful pranks are classic Orange toddler trademarks. They find immense joy in surprising others, be it by hiding toys, jumping out from hiding spots, or making funny faces just to elicit a laugh.

Eager Experimenters. For Orange infants, the world is a grand experiment. They'll drop toys to see the effects of gravity, splash in puddles to study water ripples, or mimic animal sounds just to gauge reactions. Every day is an exhilarating exploration of cause and effect.

In-the-Moment Enthusiasts. While some children might display early signs of future planning, our Orange kids are all about the here and now. They're not fretting about the snack they'll have later; they're wholly immersed in the joy of their current cookie.

Risk-Takers and Rule-Benders. Safety gates? Childproof locks? These are but minor challenges for our intrepid Orange adventurers. They often push boundaries, not out of defiance, but out of a genuine desire to explore and understand. They remind us that sometimes, rules are meant to be playfully prodded, if not outright broken.

Nurturing Nature: How Setting Shapes the Symphony of Souls

Picture this: a quaint nursery bathed in a golden glow, where the cadence of caregivers' coos and siblings' squabbles weaves a melody that caresses the tender ears of our toddling tykes. Amid the whirlwind of onesies and overalls, lullabies and laughter, the blossoming buds of temperament are gently being shaped, sculpted, and shaded. Dive with me, dear reader, into the dynamic dance of environmental enigma as we uncover how the world around whittles and waxes the wonder that is temperament.

Every touch, every tickle, every tender "there, there" from a caregiver is like the artist's brush, tenderly tinting the canvas of character. Little Lila, born with a natural Gold leaning, might become the pinnacle of punctuality if every bedtime is strictly scheduled. Or perhaps, her Gold gusto might mellow a tad, influenced by a free-spirited, Orange-oriented older sibling who insists on impromptu pajama parties past bedtime. The point? Caregivers and siblings don't merely respond to a child's temperament; they subtly shape it, steering it in a myriad of mesmerizing ways.

Now, let's muse on the magic of mirroring. When baby Benny breaks into a jubilant jig, and mommy mirrors his moves, that's not just a fun frolic fest. It's a reinforcing relay. When caregivers echo emotions, be it the jubilant jumps of joy or the tender tears of a tiny tantrum, they amplify the authenticity of the child's emotional experience. For a budding Blue Benny, this can magnify his innate empathetic essence. But for a growing Green Gina, this mirroring might moderate her analytical aloofness, adding a sprinkle of sentiment to her cognitive cocktail.

Ah, the age-old art of the "atta boy" or the "you go, girl." Positive reinforcement, that age-old ally of every parent and pedagogue. When curious Carla, with her Green glint, dismantles her toy train to understand its intricate innards and gets a high-five for her analytical acumen, we're not just celebrating curiosity. We're cementing it. The opposite, too, is equally enlightening. When adventurous Andy, our Orange offspring, attempts a daring descent down the stairs and is met with a cautionary cuddle instead of a clap, the message is clear: safety before spontaneity.

In the captivating chorus of character cultivation, genetics gifts us the notes, but the environment elicits the nuances, the crescendos, and the cadences. It's a harmonious handholding of heredity and habitat. So, as we stand on the sidelines, watching our children chart their courses, it's essential to remember our roles, not just as spectators but as sculptors, skillfully shaping the statues of their souls.

In sum, while the temperaments of Blue, Gold, Green, and Orange may be etched in early, it's the embrace of the environment that ensnares, enhances, or even eclipses these elemental endowments. And that, dear readers, is a tale as timeless as temperament itself.

The Toddler's Tapestry: Tinted but Not Typed

In the grand gallery of growing up, where every babble is a brushstroke and every toddle is a tinge of tint, there exists a masterpiece in motion—the ever-evolving enigma of early temperament. But oh, dear reader, while it might be tempting to frame this fresco forthwith, we must tread tenderly. For in the realm of rambunctious rugrats and tiny thinkers, the canvas is continually changing. Let's embark on an enlightening exploration of the elasticity of early personality, understanding the uncertainties and unveiling strategies that sing a song of support without stifling.

Imagine, if you will, little Leo. One moment, he's the embodiment of a bubbly Blue, sharing sweets and shedding sympathetic tears for a squashed snail. The next, he's all Green, gazing at the gears of a grandfather clock, pondering the passage of time. Children, like Leo, are like liquid: shapeshifting, shimmering, and sometimes, downright slippery. Recognizing the fluidity of temperament in tots is tantamount to understanding the tide—it ebbs, it flows, and just when you think you've figured it out, it surprises you with a splendid splash.

Ah, the allure of labels! How simplifying it seems to stick a Gold badge on meticulous Molly or tag tenacious Tommy as Orange. But, confining kids to categories can be a cataclysmic conundrum. While temperaments teem with telltale traits, boxing babes prematurely is akin to picking a rosebud before it blooms fully. You might just miss out on the mesmerizing multitude of colors it was destined to display. Children are not puzzles to be pieced into pre-made patterns; they're paintings that unfold in unpredictable yet unparalleled beauty.

Fear not, for while the voyage of temperament tracking teeters on the tricky, there's a compass caregivers can clutch: the nurture of nature without nailing it down. For the budding Blue, cultivate connections without curtailing their cognitive curiosities. Witnessing a Gold's gusto? Guide their grounding routines but give grace for growth and gallivanting. When you spot a glimmer of Green, spark their systematic studies but also send them to the sunny shores of spontaneity. And for the omnipresent Orange, offer outlets for their outrageous adventures but overlay opportunities for other orientations.

In the twilight of tiny years, as temperaments twinkle and twirl, the task is not to tie them down but to let them take flight. By understanding the undulating undercurrents and ushering in an understanding unburdened by unfounded ultimatums, we can champion our children to chart their courses. Whether they blossom into a brilliant Blue, go on to gleam Gold, gravitate towards Green, or oscillate in an Orange orbit, our role remains radiant and resolute: to nurture, nourish, and never negate the nascent narratives of their natures.

The Symphony of Souls: Celebrating Every Child's Chorus

As our journey through the jubilant jungles of juvenile temperaments jubilantly juxtaposes its conclusion, it's time for a poignant pause, a reflective reverie, if you will. The canvas of childhood, with its compelling cavalcade of colors—the blissful Blues, the gleaming Golds, the gratifying Greens, and the outstanding Oranges—isn't just an abstract art piece. It's a sonorous symphony, each note narrating a novel story, each chord chronicling a cherished child's character.

Dive deep into the annals of antiquity or the pages of the present, and one truth triumphantly towers: Diversity is the dynamo that drives our domain. Much like the myriad melodies in a magnum opus, the value of understanding and recognizing the unique temperament of each tiny tot is tantamount to appreciating every aria in an opera. When we witness a child's inherent inclinations without imposition, we're not just bystanders; we become benefactors of their burgeoning brilliance.

Remember little Lila? The one who'd paint rainbows even on rainy days, reflecting her radiant Blue nature? Or tenacious Timmy, whose Gold glimmers guided him to gather his toys with a gusto rarely glimpsed in his age group? How about genius Gina, whose Green-tinged games gave away her gravitation towards the grand and the logical? And don't forget our audacious Andy, forever flitting from one fantastic feat to the next, his Orange aura obvious to all observant onlookers. Each epitomizes the essence of understanding individuality in infancy.

For the marvelous maestros—the caregivers and educators orchestrating these opuses—here lies the luminous lesson: to serenade these souls with support, not stifle them with stereotypes. It's a dance of delicate dynamics, where the tune isn't dictated but discerned, where the rhythm isn't regimented but realized.

Imagine, if you will, a garden. In this garden, the Blue blossoms bloom with empathy, the Gold grains ground the terrain, the Green grasses grace us with growth, and the Orange orchids oscillate with originality. As caregivers, our role isn't to regiment the roses or orchestrate the orchids but to provide the perfect potpourri of patience, passion, and purpose.

As the curtain cascades on our captivating chronicle, one rhapsodic refrain resounds: Celebrate the child, not just the category. By championing their unique chorus, by being the background beat to their burgeoning ballads, we don't just encourage; we empower. We don't merely mentor; we marvel.

To every educator echoing these ethics, to every caregiver championing this cause—here's a heartwarming hurrah. For in your hands lies the harmonious hymn of the future, in your guidance, the grandeur of the next generation. So, here's to the Blues, the Golds, the Greens, and the Oranges—and to the symphony they compose, melodic and wonderfully expressive.

Chapter 9

Observing the Behaviors of Children: Ages 4-7

Embark on a vibrant voyage through the dynamic domain of early childhood, where personalities begin to flourish and distinctive dispositions take center stage. This chapter dives into the delightful and sometimes perplexing world of 4 to 8-year-olds, shedding light on the evolving temperaments that color their interactions, choices, and emotions.

Decoding the Dynamic World of Early Childhood: Behaviors, Motives, and Beyond

The early childhood phase, often characterized by boundless curiosity and energetic exploration, is also marked by a cognitive landscape that's still unfurling. Children aged 4 to 7, our spirited "Budding Explorers", are like sponges, absorbing information, mimicking behaviors, and testing boundaries. However, one significant limitation during this phase is their ability to introspect and define their own personality in terms of complex constructs like the Blue, Gold, Green, and Orange temperaments.

Let's delve deeper into the cognitive canvas of these young minds. At this age, the brain is still in a rapid state of development. The frontal cortex, responsible for higher-order processing like introspection, reflection, and abstract thinking, is still maturing. These children are just beginning to navigate the world of concrete operations in Piaget's stages of cognitive development, where logic is applied, but largely to tangible situations. Abstract concepts like identifying oneself as a "Green" or understanding the deeper nuances of being a "Blue" are still beyond their cognitive reach.

Furthermore, young children (and far too many adults) typically possess an egocentric perspective. This means they see the world primarily from their own viewpoint and find it challenging to consider situations from another's perspective. Asking them to introspect and assign themselves a personality type is like asking a fish to describe water—it's so intrinsic to their experience that they lack the distance or perspective to define it.

So, if children at this stage can't directly tell us about their temperamental tendencies, how can caregivers glean insights into their budding personalities? The answer lies in observation, patience, and a deep understanding of the "why" behind behaviors.

For instance, a child consistently sharing toys might not just be showcasing a learned behavior but could be exhibiting the empathetic underpinnings of the Blue temperament. Similarly, a child who revels in the routine, perhaps insisting on the same bedtime story every night, might be channeling the structure-loving nature of a Gold personality.

But merely observing behaviors isn't enough. The same behavior can be instigated by different motives, motives that are often unique for each temperament. It's crucial for parents and guardians to look beyond the action and dive deep into the motivations driving them. Why did Sarah, usually so gentle, suddenly snatch a toy from her friend? Why does Jake prefer playing with building blocks, focusing intently on creating intricate structures? Understanding the "why" helps reveal the values, desires, and fears that underpin actions. It's this foundational motive that can offer a clearer window into a child's temperament, rather than the behavior itself.

Gentle Ways to Understand Your Child's "Why"

Understanding the "why" behind children's actions can provide invaluable insights into their personalities and motivations. However, it's crucial to approach this with gentleness and genuine curiosity, not like a grand inquisitor. Here are some non-intrusive questions parents can ask their children to try to get at their motives, as well as some possible responses for each temperament.

Open-ended Conversations. "I noticed you chose to play with the building blocks today instead of painting. Can you tell me more about that choice?"

- Blue: "Well, I thought if I made a big castle, then everyone could play together and have fun. Plus, Sarah looked lonely, and I know she likes blocks."
- Gold: "I wanted to make sure all the blocks went back to their right places. And last time I painted, I got some on my shirt. I didn't want that to happen again."
- Green: "I was trying to see how tall I could stack them before they fell over. Painting is fun, but blocks are more of a challenge."
- Orange: "I just felt like it! Tomorrow I might paint a race car, or maybe I'll make a racetrack out of blocks!"

Expressing Curiosity. "That's interesting! Why did you decide to draw the sun in the corner of the paper instead of the center?"

- Blue: "I thought the sun might be rising, and I wanted to show that everyone has a new day and new chances."
- Gold: "I always see the sun in the corner of books, and I wanted my drawing to be right and look like the ones in the storybooks."
- Green: "I thought of the paper as a scene. With the sun in the corner, there's room in the middle for other things to happen. It's more realistic that way."
- Orange: "I don't know, I just felt like it! Maybe tomorrow it'll be a moon in the center!"

Sharing Observations. "I saw you gave your cookie to Soo-Min today. I'd love to hear what made you think of doing that."

- Blue: "Soo-Min looked sad. I thought maybe sharing my cookie would make her smile."
- Gold: "Soo-Min helped me clean up the toys, so I thought it would be a nice thing to do to thank her."
- Green: "I was curious to see if she'd trade her snack with me tomorrow. It's sort of an experiment."
- Orange: "I just wasn't super hungry, and it looked like she really wanted it. Plus, now we might swap snacks sometimes!"

Validating Feelings. "You seemed really upset when we left the park earlier. Can you share what was going through your mind?"

- Blue: "I felt like I didn't get to say goodbye to my friend properly. It's important to me to make sure they know I'll miss them until we play again."
- Gold: "I didn't finish the game we were playing. I always like to finish things, and leaving in the middle made me feel uneasy."
- Green: "I was watching some ants build something, and I wanted to figure out what they were doing. Leaving meant I couldn't finish my observation."
- Orange: "I was just having so much fun, and I wasn't ready for it to end! I wish we could stay and play all day."

Story Sharing. "Remember when I told you about the time I felt scared during a thunderstorm? Your face had a similar look when we heard that loud noise today. Want to tell me about it?"

- Blue: "It reminded me of a time when a friend got hurt, and I felt scared for them. Loud noises sometimes bring that feeling back."
- Gold: "I like things to be consistent and predictable. The sudden noise was unexpected, and it startled me."
- Green: "I was trying to figure out what caused the noise and if it might happen again. I was more puzzled than scared."
- Orange: "It surprised me! But I was also a bit excited because I thought maybe something fun was happening."

Gentle Probing. "You've been wanting to wear your superhero costume a lot this week. What's special about it for you?"

- Blue: "When I wear it, I feel like I can help people and make them happy. It's not just a costume; it's like a promise to be kind and brave."
- Gold: "I wore it the day I got a star in school. So now, I feel like it's my lucky charm and wearing it might make good things happen again."
- Green: "I've been thinking of ways to improve it. Maybe add some gadgets or tools. Every time I wear it, I think of new ideas."
- Orange: "It's just so cool! I feel like I can run faster, jump higher, and have all sorts of adventures in it."

Engage in Play. While playing with them, casually ask, "Why does this toy doll always sit on the toy chair, and not on the toy bed?"

- Blue: "The doll feels comfy there, and she likes to be close to her friends on the couch. The bed is for night-time, and she doesn't want to sleep yet."
- Gold: "She sits on the chair because that's where she always sits during the day. It's her routine. Every toy has its place."
- Green: "I've noticed that the chair is just the right size for her. Plus, from there, she can see everything that's going on in the room."
- Orange: "She's waiting for the toy party to start! The chair is the best spot to be ready for all the fun."

Linking to Their Favorites. "You know how in your favorite show, Lucia always shares her toys? I saw you doing the same today. What made you think of sharing?"

- Blue: "Sharing makes my friends happy, and it feels good to see them smile. Lucia and I both like making others feel good."
- Gold: "I remember how Lucia feels happy after sharing, and I wanted to feel that too. It's also the right thing to do."
- Green: "I was thinking that if I share my toys, we can come up with more ways to play together. It's like expanding the game possibilities."
- Orange: "Sharing means more fun! Plus, when I share, my friends share their cool toys with me too."

Reframing the Question. Instead of directly asking "Why?", frame it as, "What made you think of...?" or "How did you come up with that idea?"

- Blue: "I felt it in my heart. When something feels right or kind, I just know it's a good thing to do."
- Gold: "I remembered the rules we learned, and I wanted to do things the proper way. Plus, mommy always says it's good to think of others."
- Green: "I was analyzing the situation, and it just made logical sense to me at that moment. I thought about the outcomes and benefits."
- Orange: "I just went with the flow! Sometimes, I get these fun ideas and just want to try them out."

Be Part of Their World. Dive into their imaginative play and narratives. "Oh, so Mr. Teddy Bear is the king today? What made him the ruler of the toy kingdom?"

- Blue: "Mr. Teddy Bear is kind and listens to all the other toys. He wants everyone to be happy and safe, so they chose him to be king."
- Gold: "He's the oldest and most responsible toy. Everyone respects him, and they know he will make sure all the rules are followed in the kingdom."
- Green: "Mr. Teddy Bear was able to solve the big toy dispute last week, so the council of toys made him the king. He's strategic and smart."
- Orange: "He threw the best toy party ever, and everyone loved it! So, they thought he'd be the most fun king!"

Dreamscapes and Daytime. "If your toys could talk, what do you think they'd say about how you play with them?"

- Blue: "I think they'd say they feel loved and cared for. I always make sure they are together so no one feels left out."
- Gold: "They'd probably appreciate that I keep them clean and always put them back in their places. They know they're taken care of."
- Green: "They might comment on our adventures and problem-solving quests. We always have intellectual challenges and missions."
- Orange: "They'd say every day is a new adventure! We go on wild journeys, and they never get bored."

Event Recollection. "How did you feel when that happened at the park today?"

- Blue: "It made me feel a bit sad inside. I wish everyone could play together and be happy."
- Gold: "I felt a bit uneasy because it wasn't how things usually go. I like when everyone follows the rules and gets along."
- Green: "I was curious about why it happened. I tried to understand what led to that situation so I can predict it next time."
- Orange: "At first, I was surprised, but then I thought, 'Well, that's something new!' and decided to make the best out of it."

Tale-telling. "Can you make up a story about why your teddy is feeling a little sad?"

- Blue: "Teddy was feeling lonely because his best friend, Bunny, had to visit her family in the meadow. He missed their evening stories and the warmth of Bunny's hug."
- Gold: "Teddy was sad because he remembered a time when all the toys had a gathering, and he accidentally spilled juice. Even though it was an accident, he still feels bad about it."
- Green: "There's a parallel teddy universe where they have teddy challenges. Teddy missed out on the 'Honey Jar Problem-Solving' competition because he overslept."
- Orange: "Teddy wanted to throw a fun picnic for all the toys, but it rained! So, he's waiting for the sun to come out so they can all play."

Emotion Exploration. "Your face had a big frown when that happened. Can you tell me what was going through your mind?"

- Blue: "I felt a little hurt. It's important to me that everyone is kind to each other, and that didn't feel very kind."
- Gold: "It was different from what I expected, and I was thinking about how it wasn't supposed to happen that way."
- Green: "I was trying to understand why it happened. It's like a puzzle in my head I'm trying to piece together."
- Orange: "I was surprised! I was just gearing up for a fun game, and then everything changed."

Preference Probe. "I noticed you chose the blue crayon over the red one. Is there a special reason you like the blue one more today?"

- Blue: "Blue reminds me of the calm sky and the gentle ocean waves. It feels comforting and peaceful."
- Gold: "Well, yesterday I used the red one, and today I thought it was the blue one's turn. It's only fair."
- Green: "I was thinking of drawing something that represents the sky, and blue is scientifically accurate for that."
- Orange: "Just felt like going on a blue adventure today! Tomorrow, who knows, maybe it'll be green!"

Hypotheticals. "How would you feel if we went to the beach tomorrow instead of the playground?"

- Blue: "I'd feel happy because the beach is calm, and I can listen to the waves. But I'd also miss the swings at the playground where I imagine I'm flying."
- Gold: "I'd be okay if you tell me beforehand. I like to know what's coming up. The beach sounds fun, but I've prepared my shoes for the playground."
- Green: "Interesting! The beach would give me a chance to see how the tide works. But, can we still try out my new kite there?"
- Orange: "Oh, that'd be exciting! I can run in the sand, build castles, and maybe even splash you with water!"

Activity Assessment. "What's your favorite part of our bedtime story routine? Why do you like that part the best?"

- Blue: "I love the part when we snuggle close, and you do the different voices for each character. It feels cozy and full of love."
- Gold: "It's when we recap the story from the night before. I like the continuity and remembering our routines."
- Green: "My favorite is when the story has a twist or a mystery. It gets my brain thinking even as I drift off to sleep."
- Orange: "The adventurous parts! Especially when the heroes zoom around and save the day. Makes me dream of big adventures!"

Artistic Inquiry. "That's a beautiful drawing! Can you tell me the story behind it?"

- Blue: "It's a world where everyone is friends, and there's peace everywhere. I drew this after thinking about how lovely it would be if everyone just smiled at each other."
- Gold: "Thank you! This is our family having a picnic. I remembered our last outing and thought about drawing it so we can remember it."
- Green: "It's an imaginary planet with three suns and gravity that works differently. I was wondering how shadows would look there."
- Orange: "That's my superhero land! There's action, flying cars, and every person has a superpower. It's where every day is an adventure!"

Friendship Focal Point. "You seem to enjoy playing with Jenny a lot. What's your favorite game to play together? Why is it special?"

- Blue: "Jenny and I love to play 'House.' We pretend to be in a family where everyone takes care of each other. It feels like we're sharing a piece of our hearts."
- Gold: "We have a routine! Every day, after snack time, we play 'School.' I like it because we follow the same rules, and I get to be the teacher sometimes."
- Green: "We play this game called 'Space Explorers.' We make up planets and their rules. I like it because it's always a new adventure, and Jenny has some cool ideas."
- Orange: "Oh, we play tag! It's super fun because we run around a lot, and sometimes, we change the rules to make it more challenging!"

Decision Dissection. "You decided to give some of your snack to your brother. What made you want to share with him today?"

- Blue: "I noticed he looked a bit sad, and I thought maybe sharing my snack would cheer him up. Plus, it's nice to make others feel good."
- Gold: "Well, last week he shared his cookies with me. It's only fair that I return the favor. It's our little snack-sharing tradition."
- Green: "I was thinking about how sharing can be a sort of experiment. I gave him some to see if he'd like it as much as I do. Do you think he enjoyed it?"
- Orange: "He was making those funny faces, and I thought, why not? Sharing's fun, especially when it leads to goofy snack-time moments!"

Tips for Proper Inquiries

Remember, these questions aren't about extracting information but rather fostering communication and understanding. It's crucial to ask them with genuine curiosity and without any preconceived judgments.

It's always essential to create a safe, non-judgmental space for children to express themselves. The key lies in showing genuine interest and ensuring the child feels their perspective is valued and understood. This helps foster trust and deeper emotional connection.

While our "Budding Explorers" might not have the cognitive tools to introspect and label their personalities, their actions, driven by their nascent values and motives, sing their temperamental tunes. For caregivers, the challenge and joy lie in listening, observing, and gently guiding, all while refraining from boxing them into predefined categories prematurely. After all, the journey of understanding is as beautiful as the destination.

Blue Children Aged 4 to 7

Empathetic Extensions. A distinct hallmark of Blue children in this age bracket is their heightened sense of empathy. Not limited to just sensing the moods of those close to them, they often show an uncanny ability to feel the emotions of others, even those beyond their immediate circle. It's not uncommon for a Blue child to approach a teary-eyed peer and ask, genuinely, "Are you okay? Can I help?"

Relationship Reverence. Friendship is not a mere playdate arrangement for these young souls. Instead, it's a bond, often deep and intense. They cherish their friends and can sometimes even form "soulmate" kind of relationships, where they believe in the idea of having a "best friend forever."

Storytelling and Symbolism. While storytelling is a universal childhood pastime, Blue children infuse theirs with rich emotions and layered meanings. Their tales often revolve around themes of love, friendship, kindness, and sometimes, even heartbreak and healing.

Seekers of Harmony. Even at this tender age, Blue kids despise conflict. Whether it's a disagreement on the playground or an argument between siblings at home, they often step in as peacemakers, offering solutions or sometimes even compromising their own wishes for the sake of harmony.

Intuitive Interactions. They have a knack for reading between the lines. A glance, a sigh, a subtle change in voice tone—they pick up on these nuances. This intuitive prowess means they sometimes understand things that even adults might miss.

Creativity and Color. While their creativity spans a wide spectrum, there's a distinct leaning towards activities that allow emotional expression. This could be through painting, where blue skies might depict happiness or a gray cloud might signify a sadder day.

Depth over Details. Blue children, when recounting an event or sharing an experience, often focus on how it made them feel rather than the logistical details. They might forget the name of the zoo they visited, but they'll vividly remember feeling sad for the caged bird they saw.

Affectionate and Expressive. Hugs, comforting pats, holding hands—physical displays of affection come naturally to them. It's their way of forming connections and assuring their loved ones of their feelings.

Moral Compass in Motion. Even if not explicitly taught, Blue kids show a budding moral compass. They're the ones who get genuinely troubled if a friend cheats in a game or if they feel someone has been wronged.

Teachers and Healers. Play-pretend often gives children away, and with Blue kids, they frequently take on roles of teachers, caregivers, or healers. Whether it's nursing a "sick" toy back to health or teaching their stuffed animals about love and friendship, their play patterns echo their innate drive to nurture and enlighten.

Gold Children Aged 4 to 7

Routine Relishers. The world of a Gold child is one of patterns and predictability. Whether it's adhering to a bedtime ritual, a morning routine, or even the way they arrange their toys, consistency is key. Their love for the familiar means they often find comfort in routines that might seem monotonous to others.

Trust and Loyalty. Loyalty isn't just an adult concept for these young Golds. Once they bond with a friend, they are often steadfast in their allegiance. They remember promises, value trust, and take umbrage if someone breaks a pact, even if it's as simple as a playground promise.

Emerging Responsibility. It's not uncommon to find a Gold child reminding their peers to follow rules or even chiding them gently for not adhering to them. They take on roles like class helpers or line leaders with utmost seriousness, viewing them not as mere titles but responsibilities.

Guardians of Fairness. "It's not fair!" might be a refrain you'll hear often if things don't seem just. These children have an innate sense of right and wrong, and they believe in the importance of everyone getting an equal shot.

Planning and Preparation. Spontaneity isn't their strongest suit. A Gold child prefers to know what's coming next. They might ask about plans for the weekend on a Monday or discuss what they'll do for their next birthday even if it's months away.

Memory Mavens. Gold children are often the keepers of family traditions and memories. They'll remind parents of that specific bedtime story they read last winter or the annual family picnic spot, emphasizing the importance of upholding these traditions.

Organized Outings. Play for them often mirrors the structured world they adore. You'll find them organizing their toys into categories, setting up orderly games, or even arranging their drawings chronologically.

Honesty as a Hallmark. Telling the truth, even when it's uncomfortable, is a typical trait of Gold children. They believe in honesty and can sometimes be painfully straightforward with their observations and opinions.

Seeking Approval and Appreciation. A pat on the back, a word of praise—these mean the world to them. They thrive on recognition and often look for validation that they're on the right track, be it in tasks or behavior.

Care and Concern. Gold children often display a nurturing side, especially towards those younger or weaker. They might take a younger sibling or friend under their wing, guiding them through the nuances of a game or sharing wisdom about "big kid" stuff. Their caregiving streak is an early indication of the protective and responsible individuals they're growing into.

Green Children Aged 4 to 7

Question Quotient. The world of a Green child is a universe of wonderment waiting to be deciphered. "Why is the sky blue?", "How does the TV work?", "What makes the car move?"—their inquisitiveness knows no bounds.

Every observation spins into a query, each more intricate than the last.

Puzzle Proclivity. Lay a jigsaw puzzle or a brain teaser in front of them, and watch their eyes light up. For Green children, puzzles aren't just games; they're challenges. They'll painstakingly piece them together, enjoying not just the end result but the journey of discovery.

Fact Fanatics. An affinity for factual information is evident. They'll surprise you with tidbits about dinosaurs, space, or even how household gadgets work. This love for knowledge often leads them to voraciously read or engage with educational materials way above their grade level.

Focused and Unfazed. Once engrossed in a task, these children display an almost laser-like focus. External distractions seldom deter them. Whether they're building a complex Lego structure or deep diving into an interactive science experiment, their commitment is unwavering.

Early Strategists. Board or computer games involving strategy, like chess or even simplified versions of it, captivate them. They're not just playing; they're plotting, planning, predicting—every move calculated with foresight.

Complex Conversations. Their discussions, even with peers, often touch upon intricate subjects. You might overhear a debate about the fastest animal, the vastness of the universe, or the mechanics behind a swinging pendulum.

Emotionally Reserved. While they're a whirlwind of cognitive activity, Green children might sometimes seem distant or reserved, especially in emotionally charged situations. They're processing feelings in their unique analytical manner, often preferring to mull over matters before sharing.

Innovative Implementers. Hand them standard toys, and they'll find unconventional ways to use them. Building blocks might become the foundation for a makeshift pulley system or a vehicle with intricate modifications.

Peer Preferences. While they play and engage with all, Green kids often gravitate towards older children or even adults, finding their conversations more stimulating. They relish the opportunity to learn from these interactions, quenching their insatiable thirst for knowledge.

Self-Paced Learners. They prefer to learn at their rhythm, often delving deep into subjects of interest while glossing over others. This selectivity isn't defiance but an innate desire to explore topics that genuinely resonate with their analytical minds. Their love for autonomy in learning makes them pioneers of their educational journey.

Orange Children Aged 4 to 7

Ebullient Explorers. Orange children embrace the world with open arms and boundless enthusiasm. Whether they're scaling the jungle gym with fearless gusto or dashing through the yard with wind-swept hair, their zest for life is unmistakable. Every corner turned holds a new adventure, and they're eager to unearth it.

Immediacy is Key. Patience might not be their strongest suit. When an Orange child says, "I want to do it now," they genuinely mean now. Whether it's a game, a treat, or a new activity, they're driven by the present moment's thrill.

Sensory Seekers. Textures, tastes, sounds—Orange kids thrive on sensory experiences. You'll find them building sandcastles, relishing the grainy feel, or splashing in puddles, delighting in the cool splash. Their world is a carnival of sensations, each more intriguing than the last.

Social Butterflies. Their charisma and high energy often make them the life of any kiddie party. They naturally gravitate towards group activities and often emerge as the informal leaders, rallying their peers with infectious enthusiasm.

Flexibility in Flow. Change isn't a challenge for these young ones; it's just another flavor of fun. They adapt with ease, moving seamlessly from one activity to another. While they cherish their routines, they're hardly ever flustered when things don't go as planned.

Risk-takers and Trailblazers. While they're safety-conscious, Orange children aren't afraid to push boundaries. Be it attempting a new acrobatic trick on the swing or venturing into a more challenging board game, they're always up for the test.

Storytellers Supreme. Their vivid imaginations birth the most riveting tales. Dragons, superheroes, intergalactic explorers—their narratives are a delightful blend of fantasy and reality, always narrated with dramatic flair.

Hands-on Learners. They're not just listeners; they're doers. Orange children learn best when they're actively involved. Touch, trial, and sometimes error are their preferred pedagogies.

Champions of Choice. Empower them with options and watch their eyes sparkle. Whether it's choosing the day's outfit (even if it's a superhero cape with rain boots) or picking a weekend activity, they cherish the autonomy and often make decisions with surprising decisiveness.

Affectionate and Affable. Their large hearts match their vast energy reserves. An Orange child is quick to offer a hug, share a toy, or console a friend. Their warmth is genuine, and their friendships, though often numerous, are heartfelt. They navigate the social seas of childhood with both enthusiasm and empathy, making waves and friends wherever they roam.

Teaching Your Children About Colors

Now that you understand what each color looks like and thinks like, we might want to take this new understanding up a notch and invite our children to take a vivid voyage of versatile virtue and teach the tempering tints to our tiny tots. We encourage you to embark on an enlightening escapade into the world of temperaments. For between the intriguing ages of 4 to 7, lies a golden opportunity—an age where imagination intertwines with awakening awareness. Here, we find a prime period to introduce our cherubs to the colors of character: Blue, Gold, Green, and Orange.

Ah, but why, you might ask, should one embark on this chromatic quest with children so young? Read on, for the tale is both entertaining and enlightening!

1. Amplifying Self-Awareness. Imagine a world where your little Liam understands that his heartwarming hugs and comforting coos are reflective of his dominant Blue temperament. This awareness isn't about boxing him into a category, but rather empowering him to embrace his innate strengths and understand the motive behind his moves.

2. Cultivating Compassion. When young Ella realizes that her brother Ethan's meticulous arranging of toys isn't just a quirky behavior, but a reflection of his Gold temperament, she learns to appreciate differences. And thus, the seeds of compassion and understanding sprout.

3. Prepping for Peer Interactions. School is the proverbial melting pot of personalities. Introducing temperaments early on equips children with tools to understand their classmates better. Imagine if Lucas, with his fiery Orange energy, realizes his friend Sarah's contemplative questions arise from her Green temperament. Harmony ensues!

4. Confidence in Colors. Knowing one's temperament is akin to having a secret superpower. When kids understand why they feel or act a certain way, it reinforces confidence in their choices and reduces self-doubt.

5. Flexibility and Fluidity. Introducing kids to all four temperaments ensures they don't pigeonhole themselves. It fosters flexibility, encouraging them to tap into their secondary or tertiary colors when needed. Little Isabelle might be predominantly Green, but she can channel her inner Gold when organizing her bookshelf.

6. Strengthening Bonds. A shared language of temperaments can serve as a bridge between parents and kids. It's not just about kids understanding themselves, but also about parents gaining insights into their children's worlds.

7. Building Resilience. Understanding that not everyone operates from the same temperament palette equips children with the resilience to face conflicts. It's not personal; it's just a different shade of interaction!

8. Crafting Creativity. Knowledge of different temperaments can stimulate creativity. Storytime can be peppered with characters embodying various temperaments, making tales more engaging and enlightening.

9. A Foothold for the Future. By understanding the spectrum of temperaments early on, children are better prepared to navigate the diverse personalities they'll encounter in their future academic and professional lives.

10. Celebrating Uniqueness. At the heart of this chromatic journey is the celebration of individuality. Understanding temperaments teaches children that every color, every shade, is essential to the grand canvas of life.

To put it succinctly, weaving the world of temperaments into your child's early education is like gifting them a magical map. It's a guide that helps them navigate the vast landscapes of personalities, ensuring they cherish their color while appreciating the entire spectrum. In this vibrant voyage, every hue holds a lesson, every shade a story. And oh, what a vivid tale it is! Here's a story of what happened after one six-year old girl was taught about the four temperaments by her parents.

A Real-Life Example of Color Shifting

Learning about colors gave Tina a profound epiphany. She stumbled upon her mother's art supplies one day and saw the vast array of colored pencils. Tina decided she was no longer just one color but a magnificent blend of them all! Taking a cue from her newfound spectrum of personality hues, she began dressing in a different color each day of the week. Monday was her Blue day, filled with empathy as she consoled her stuffed animals after the trauma of being left alone all night. Tuesdays were Gold, where order reigned supreme, and every toy had its meticulous place.

But things took an amusing turn on Wednesday. Wednesdays were her Green days. In her pursuit of knowledge, Tina dismantled her father's alarm clock to understand its inner workings. While her sense of curiosity was certainly commendable, her timing was questionable. Her father overslept and, in a flustered state, wore mismatched shoes to work!

By Thursday, her Orange spontaneity took over. The family's living room turned into a wild obstacle course. Cushions were strewn around as steppingstones over imaginary lava, chairs toppled to create makeshift tunnels, and the couch became the final fortress.

On Friday, she revisited Blue, but with a twist. Watching a bird outside her window, she was overwhelmed with such a swell of compassion that she decided it must be cold and tried to bring it inside for some warm cocoa.

That, of course, led to some frantic flapping, a toppling vase, and a bewildered cat joining the chase!

Over the weekend, Tina combined all her colors. She sketched out a heartfelt card for her parents (Blue), organized her art supplies (Gold), pondered on the mysteries of the universe, like why ice cream always disappears so quickly from her bowl (Green), and surprised her family with an impromptu indoor picnic (Orange).

Monday morning, Tina's mother found a note pinned to Tina's dresser: "Today, I am a Rainbow!" she declared. While Tina's week-long colorful escapade brought laughter, minor chaos, and some unforgettable moments, it beautifully encapsulated a child's journey of self-exploration. Like the myriad personalities we juggle throughout life, Tina embraced them all, reminding us that sometimes, we need to paint outside the lines to truly appreciate the masterpiece that is our unique self. And in Tina's world, every day could be a new shade of wonderful.

Chapter 10

Measuring the Personality of Older Children

Navigate through the intricate world of personality with this enlightening chapter, which explains where personality comes from and how to identify the temperament of your children during their first 18 years.

Formal Ways to Measure Personality

Up to this point in this book, we have examined the informal and intuitive ways we can try to identify the personality styles of our infants and young children. However, it's time for an exciting pivot: we're going to shift and help our children identify their own personality preferences with a formal psychometric assessment.

The realization of one's own personality is a journey that intertwines with the intricate process of brain development and maturation. The ability to distinguish one's own identity emerges gradually. It requires a certain level of cognitive independence to understand one's preferences and innate tendencies separate from the influences of external entities such as parents, teachers, siblings, and friends.

Developmental psychologists underscore the pivotal age of 8 as a cornerstone in this developmental trajectory when children begin to be accountable for their choices and start to experience autonomy. It is around this age that the neural substrates of a child's brain have burgeoned to a point where self-perception begins to decouple from external judgements and influences, thereby enabling them to comprehend and interpret their own personality tendencies with relative accuracy.

The journey through understanding one's personality is not just a singular path but a multi-tiered exploration, adapting to the various cognitive and linguistic stages of development across different ages.

The next five chapters contain carefully curated assessments that you can administer to children of distinct age and developmental ranges: 8-9, 10-11, 12-13, 14-15, and 16-17-year-olds.

Each assessment has been meticulously crafted with words and concepts that make sense to each age group, considering the cognitive and linguistic capabilities pertinent to each bracket. This will help ensure an engaging and accessible exploration for every child and teen.

These assessments, which are comprised of 24 straightforward questions with a simple A or B response, have been designed to gently guide your progeny through a journey of self-exploration while maintaining a manageable cognitive load.

While navigating through these assessments, your role as a parent is to administer the test and interpret the results, allowing your child the autonomy to choose the answers that resonate most with them. As the administrator, you will read the questions to your child, but always let them be the ones to identify their answer. You may disagree with their responses based on your years of observation, but that is okay. Make a silent note to yourself about the discrepancy and let them proceed with their perceptions.

The assessments have been labeled with specific age ranges. However, every child matures at a unique pace, and their cognitive, emotional, and linguistic developments don't always align seamlessly with their chronological age. Feel free to administer whichever test is most appropriate for your youngster.

As you guide your child through the assessments, attentively observe whether they are struggling with the words or concepts due to the version's simplicity or complexity. If this is the case, gently transition them to explore another version. This adaptive approach ensures that the exploration of their primary colors unfolds as a delightful, enlightening, and validating adventure, free from unintended hurdles or labels.

For those parents with children who have blossomed beyond the age of 17, that particular version would still probably work, although it steers away from such topics as finances, intimacy, stressors, liabilities, anxiety, and other aspects that adults have to deal with and which are measureable. For most adults, we encourage the utilization of our standard adult assessments (not found in this book), which rather than being a dichotomous AB format, more often involves the more cognitively challenging task of ranking or rating a more extensive list of questions.

Facilitating a continuing exploration into the vibrant world of personality is a worthy goal of any child or adult. Through this colorful journey, may each individual discover not only the beauty in their own unique hue but also develop an appreciation for the diverse spectrum of colors that adorn our world.

The Evolving Spectrum

Embarking on the vibrant journey of personality development unveils a spectrum where the primary color takes precedence, forming the foundational hue from which our character is significantly shaded. Much like the tadpole who is genetically destined to mature into a frog, or an eft who, if not eaten by birds, reptiles, and other amphibians, will grow up to be a newt—despite the variables in our environment, our fundamental primary color remains a steadfast component of our being, guiding our core responses and perspectives throughout life.

In the initial years of childhood, personal worlds often collide with those of others, especially within the diversified environment of a school. In this realm, children undertake an exploration and comparative analysis as they witness a myriad of behaviors, values, and perspectives exhibited by their peers. This exposure to a varied palette of personality colors, each differentiating individual personalities, becomes a vital component of their social development.

Children often gravitate towards friendships with peers reflecting similar personality colors, finding comfort, resonance, and a reassuring echo in shared intrinsic behaviors and values. This tendency provides a stable, familiar backdrop against which they can safely navigate the complexities of social interaction and understanding.

As youngsters mature and establish a comfortable understanding of their own personality, children may begin to forge relationships with those who embody complementary temperaments (Blue with Gold or Orange, Gold with Blue or Green, Green with Gold or Orange, and Orange with Blue or Green) or even opposite temperaments (Blue and Green, or Gold and Orange). This expansion in social connection often notably emerges during early adolescence, a period marked by both exploration and consolidation of personal and social identity.

Let me share an anecdote that embodies this concept. Once, at a summer camp, the counselors taught the concept of personality colors to the 10-year old campers as an ice-breaker activity. The next day, one of the counselors organized an art activity where the children were to paint their "spirit animals." Timmy, a particularly exuberant child, declared, "I'm a parrot!" He then proceeded to paint not one, not two, but four, each a shade of Blue, Gold, Green, and Orange. When questioned about his colorful ensemble, he nonchalantly replied, "Well, today, I feel like a Blue parrot, but who knows? Tomorrow, I might be feeling particularly Gold." As the camp days progressed, true to his words, his daily activities reflected the parrot shade of the day. Blue parrot days saw Timmy narrating imaginative tales, while on Gold parrot days, he was found meticulously arranging his art supplies. It was a lively, illustrative lesson on how children navigate their emerging personalities.

During adolescence, particularly between the ages of 12 and 14, individuals often sail into a phase of experimental exploration, propelled by the rollercoaster of developmental and social changes inherent to this stage of life. This may involve a temporary wavering of the stability of their primary color as they "try on" different hues, navigating a kaleidoscopic array of personalities in a quest to "find themselves." However, even after dabbling in various shades and exploring different temperaments, most eventually retreat back, realigning with their dominant color which intrinsically governs their core reactions and perceptions. This alignment underscores the influential and enduring impact of our primary color, even amidst the fluctuations and explorations of developmental growth.

Here's another story that explains what this might look like in real life.

The Mood Board Experiment

Jamie, ever the Blue, adored her world of crafts. Her room was a sanctuary of emotions and creativity, with mood boards filled with cutouts, quotes, and fabric swatches. Each board represented a different emotion, curated intricately by Jamie, reflecting her insights into human feelings.

Her brother Sam, a quintessential Green, was her polar opposite. Rather than indulging in emotions, he indulged in analytics. His tablet was filled with graphs, and he had an app for every experiment. The siblings, although close, had distinctly different worlds.

There was an upcoming science fair at the school and Jamie had no intention of entering it—that was something far more suited to Sam. One day, as Jamie was curating a new mood board titled "Serenity," she had an idea. What if she could create an experiment out of her mood boards, understanding how different colors and textures evoked varied emotions in people? She thought of Sam and his love for data. This could be a perfect blend of their worlds!

Excitedly, she pitched the idea to Sam, suggesting they survey people's reactions to different mood boards. Each board would represent a different emotion, and participants would record their feelings after viewing each. To Sam, this was a delightful proposal—a chance to gather and analyze real-world data!

The siblings converted a corner of their shared study into "The Mood Corner." While Jamie designed the boards, Sam created a digital survey. They invited friends and family to participate, explaining the experiment and then watching as each person reacted to the different boards.

The "Mood Board Experiment," as they dubbed it, provided fascinating insights. People often felt the intended emotion but sometimes with variations. The "Serenity" board, for example, evoked feelings of nostalgia in some or even a touch of sadness in others.

The school science fair became the perfect platform to showcase their unique project. Their exhibit attracted many—some drawn by the colors and textures of Jamie's boards and others intrigued by Sam's detailed analytics.

The experiment was more than just a project; it was a synthesis of the Blue and Green worlds. Jamie learned the value of structured feedback, and Sam experienced the abstract nature of emotions.

While Jamie continued her artistic endeavors after the fair, she now had a new tool in her arsenal: analytical insight. And Sam, often seen with a new mood board in his room, had found a colorful way to understand human emotions.

Growing Up Through the Colors of Personality

Growing up is a colorful adventure, much like flipping through a well-illustrated storybook. Remember when Jamie, our little Blue enthusiast, suddenly took an interest in the school's science fair, even though she'd never shown a smidgen of interest in science before? It's all about exploration and testing out different shades of our personalities as we mature.

As kids grow into young adults, they often start appreciating the diverse flavors of personalities around them. It's like they've been enjoying vanilla ice cream all their life and suddenly discover there's also chocolate, strawberry, and mint! They might still love vanilla best, but occasionally they want a bite of something else. That's them venturing into the shades of their secondary or even tertiary personality colors.

Now, when they step into the tricky teenage years and early adulthood, these kids, now almost grown-ups, often find themselves trying on different personality hats. It's their way of handling the countless challenges they meet. Just like how we adults sometimes switch between being the strict parent, the fun friend, or the focused employee, based on what the situation demands.

Yet, through all this, their primary personality color, that very first scoop of ice cream they fell in love with, remains their go-to flavor. It's their comfort zone, their natural reflex. Even if they sometimes choose to swirl it with a bit of chocolate or top it with some fruit, vanilla is still the main ingredient.

And that's the beauty of it. Our personality is a spectrum. It shifts, it swirls, but it always has that core essence. It's not just about the traits we're born with but also about the experiences we gather, the friendships we form, and the challenges we overcome.

In essence, growing up is all about adding more colors to our personality palette. We start with our primary shade, then dab a bit of this and a touch of that, creating a masterpiece as we move through life's many phases. It's about learning, adapting, and always being the best version of ourselves, no matter which shade we choose to showcase.

The Five Versions of the Primary Color Quiz

The formal assessments found in the following five chapters have been meticulously crafted to compare each primary color against every other, doing so an equal number of times to ensure a uniform distribution of comparisons. Furthermore, careful attention has been dedicated to balancing the positioning of each color, whether in the A or B spot, to minimize order effects. To circumvent redundancy, each question probes a distinct facet of personality. Finally, questions within each version are randomized to reduce predictability, prevent memorization, reduce bias, increase reliability, and enhance external validity.

Primary Color Quiz: Ages 8-9 embraces straightforward content, language, and structural simplicity. Tailoring to approximately 2nd to 4th-grade levels, the quiz avoids complex vocabulary and sentence structures to ensure accessibility and comprehension for its target age and grade demographic. This strategic simplicity encourages independent engagement from children, fostering a direct and uncomplicated quiz-taking experience.

Primary Color Quiz: Ages 10-11 introduces a sprinkle of complexity with words like "spontaneous," "hypotheses," and "adrenaline." These choices may be particularly resonant and stimulating for those in the 5th to 6th-grade bracket. Although slightly more challenging, the quiz remains potentially accessible and enjoyable for younger children boasting advanced reading skills, especially with adult guidance.

Primary Color Quiz: Ages 12-13 is penned in an accessible yet mildly nuanced style, assuming a reading level approximate to grades 7-8. The words used in the questions and statements are not exceedingly complex and should be within or slightly above the average vocabulary of a 12 to 13-year-old. The concepts explored, like enjoying adventure, respecting rules, and valuing friendship, are things that many 12 to 13-year-olds have likely encountered in their own lives or in school. The statements are fairly concise and should not present a significant reading challenge in terms of length or complexity.

Primary Color Quiz: Ages 14-15 utilizes a language and sentence structure that is relatively straightforward and transparent. This implies a reading level apt for middle to high school students. Steering clear from complex vocabulary and intricate sentence structures, the quiz assures a digestible and undemanding reading experience, facilitating ease and engagement throughout the personality exploration.

Primary Color Quiz: Ages 16-17 is designed for students in the 11th or 12th school year. It adheres to clear and succinct sentence construction, coupled with straightforward instructions, ensuring that it doesn't entangle participants in complex vocabulary or technical jargon. Some teenagers, especially those with advanced reading capabilities, might perceive it as overly simplistic, potentially prompting a transition towards an adult assessment for a more cognitively challenging experience that involves ranking questions.

Chapter 11

Primary Color Quiz: Ages 8-9

In this chapter, we introduce a straightforward assessment designed specifically for 8 to 9-year-olds to pinpoint their dominant temperament. The findings are then presented in a report, highlighting key character traits and patterns, crafted with a 3rd to 4th-grade reading level for easy comprehension.

Explanation

This assessment is **not** designed to be self-administered as are our adult assessments. You, as the parent or guardian, will read the instructions to your child, ask them all 24 questions, and record and tally their results.

Your child will listen and pick their favorite results. Make sure to keep it light and fun. Remind them that there are no wrong answers, only fun discoveries!

Begin by reading the instructions found below. If you choose to give your own instructions, please make sure to keep your tone light and friendly. Remind them that there are no wrong answers, only fun discoveries!

Next, read the A or B options for each question, making sure to give your child a moment to think and choose. *Don't read the colors in parenthesis, those are for your use in the scoring process.*

As they answer a question, on a spare piece of paper you can write down the four colors, Blue, Gold, Green, and Orange and then make a tally mark next to the color every time they choose that color. There is also a scoring box at the end of the assessment if you want to use it.

After the 24 questions have been answered, tally up the number of times they chose each color and record it. The highest number is their primary color. The next highest score may hint at their secondary color, but this type of AB test is not designed to measure their complete spectrum, just their primary color.

There is a summary at the end of each assessment for all four temperaments. Feel free to share that with your child. It is written at their reading level. They may also benefit from learning about the other three colors and trying to figure out the personality type of their family and friends.

Instructions

> TO BE READ BY PARENT TO CHILD

It's time for an adventure! Welcome to the Primary Color Quiz, a magical journey where we'll find out which color—Blue, Gold, Green, or Orange—shines just like you! Are you excited to find out? Let's have some fun together!

I will read some fun questions to you. Every question will have two options: an A and a B. I'll read them both to you, and you get to decide which one sounds more like something you'd say, think, or do! Sometimes both might seem a bit like you, and that's perfectly okay—just choose the one that feels a teeny bit more like you!

Here's a super-duper important secret: Be wonderfully you! There are no wrong answers here, so pick the one that makes your heart happy, not the one you think your friends would pick.

No need to rush—let's take it easy and enjoy every single question. Think about your answer, but also remember, your very first thought is super valuable! So don't worry about thinking too hard.

Guess what? This is a fun game, not homework! So let's giggle, think, and enjoy every question. We're here to explore what makes you the awesome kid you are!

After all the questions, we'll look at your answers together and find out which color twinkles just like you! Ready to find your special color and sprinkle some fun around? Let's get started on our colorful adventure!

Primary Color Quiz

	A	B
1	I like making sure all my toys are put away. (Gold)	I enjoy comforting a friend who is upset. (Blue)
2	I wonder how plants make their own food. (Green)	I like to have a plan before starting a game. (Gold)
3	I love imagining I am a pirate on an adventure. (Orange)	I enjoy drawing pictures with my friends. (Blue)
4	I like playing fast and exciting games. (Orange)	I enjoy learning about how the Earth moves. (Green)
5	I like to play games without knowing the rules. (Orange)	I believe in being honest and true. (Gold)
6	I enjoy playing pretend with wild stories. (Orange)	I like understanding how machines work. (Green)
7	I like to do things in a certain, organized way. (Gold)	I'm curious about how animals live in the wild. (Green)
8	I like helping people work out disagreements. (Blue)	I enjoy being praised for doing things correctly. (Gold)

9	I like telling stories that make people happy. (Blue)	I like figuring out what makes the weather change. (Green)
10	I believe it's important to follow the rules. (Gold)	I enjoy singing songs to express my feelings. (Blue)
11	I like talking about how my day went. (Blue)	I like being on the move and exploring. (Orange)
12	I like making new friends and being kind. (Blue)	I love trying things even if I might make mistakes. (Orange)
13	I like to make lists to remember things. (Gold)	I'm curious about why the sky is blue. (Green)
14	I like watching shows about space and planets. (Green)	I feel good when my room is neat and tidy. (Gold)
15	I like to ask lots of questions about the world. (Green)	I like listening and giving advice to my friends. (Blue)
16	I enjoy reading facts about dinosaurs. (Green)	I enjoy acting out fun and silly stories. (Orange)
17	I like to listen and understand my friends' feelings. (Blue)	I believe in finishing my homework on time. (Gold)

18	I like to be recognized for following instructions. (Gold)	I like to surprise people with fun things to do without planning ahead. (Orange)
19	I like to create art to show my love to my family. (Blue)	I like inventing things using my knowledge. (Green)
20	I like making sure I am always on time. (Gold)	I love discovering new paths and places. (Orange)
21	I like making up new and exciting games. (Orange)	I like sharing interesting stories with my friends. (Blue)
22	I enjoy being wild and free in my play. (Orange)	I like to keep my promises to my friends. (Gold)
23	I like reading books about different creatures in the sea. (Green)	I love doing things without a set plan. (Orange)
24	I like exploring and understanding how things are made. (Green)	I like being there for a friend in need. (Blue)

Great job completing the quiz! We hope you had fun learning about yourself. Remember, everyone is special and unique in their own way. Keep being awesome and continue exploring the wonderful person you are!

Scoring

Count the Blue Answers. Begin by reviewing the answers and count every instance where the color Blue was selected. Write down the total number in the Blue box below.

Repeat for Each Color. Use the same process to tally the selections for Gold, Green, and Orange. Make sure to keep track of each color's total separately to avoid any confusion.

Identifying the Dominant Color. Identify which color has the highest total number—that color is most representative of your child's personality according to the quiz.

BLUE	GOLD	GREEN	ORANGE

The Blue Personality

- I love making new friends because caring about others makes me happy!
- When other people are happy or sad, I feel that way too because their feelings matter to me.
- I like to give big, warm hugs and make sure everyone is feeling really good and happy.
- Sharing my toys and snacks with my friends is fun because it makes them smile!
- I'm a great listener and love hearing stories about my friends' days and adventures.
- Saying "I'm sorry" is important to me because I don't like seeing anyone upset or hurt.
- I enjoy writing little notes or drawing pictures to show my friends and family I care about them.
- Being honest and always telling the truth is super important to me.
- If you're feeling down, I'll be the one who notices and asks if you're okay.
- I like to help out at home or in class without being asked because it's nice to be helpful.
- Sometimes I might need extra hugs and comforting words because my feelings can be really tender.
- Playing games is fun and I make sure everyone is having a good time, not just focusing on winning.
- If you tell me a secret, I promise to keep it safe and not tell anyone.
- Spending lots of time with my friends and family makes me feel close and connected to them.
- Writing in a diary is fun for me because I can express all my important feelings.

- Talking about feelings is interesting and I like to know how you feel too.
- If there's a disagreement, I'll try to help solve it by talking and making sure everyone is happy afterward.
- Sometimes, even if I'm feeling sad, I try to smile so I don't make others feel sad too.
- Saying "I love you" to my family and friends is special and I say it with my whole heart.
- Doing nice things, like making a card or helping out, is my way of spreading kindness.
- I like giving compliments, like saying your drawing is nice, because I love to make you smile!
- Asking you how you are is my way of showing that I really, really care about you.
- When I say "thank you" or "please," I really mean it because being polite is kind.
- If I make a promise, I'll do my very best to keep it because it's important to be reliable.
- Planning little parties or playdates is exciting because being with friends is a bunch of fun for me!

The Gold Personality

- I like having a plan for the day, so I know what fun things are coming up!
- My room is neat and tidy because I know where everything is and it looks nice.
- I feel happy when everything goes as planned and there are no big surprises.
- Doing my homework before playing is important so I can enjoy playtime without worrying.
- I respect the rules and think they help everyone get along better.
- Being on time matters to me because it's respectful and makes the day go smoothly.
- When I say I will do something, you can count on me to do it because keeping promises is really important.
- I like to help others and often volunteer to assist, whether it's in class or at home.
- Having a list of things to do makes me feel organized and prepared.
- When playing games, I think following the rules makes it fair and fun for everyone!
- I get my chores done without being reminded because I know it's my responsibility.
- Making sure my friends and family are okay and safe is something I always think about.
- I often remember people's birthdays and enjoy picking out thoughtful gifts.
- Being in charge and helping lead the group in a game or activity is fun and exciting for me.
- I really appreciate when things are fair and everyone gets a turn.

- I show respect by listening carefully when others are talking and waiting my turn to speak.
- I'm good at saving my allowance because I like to plan for something special later on.
- If I start a project, like a big puzzle or a drawing, I like to finish it before moving to the next thing.
- Celebrating holidays and traditions is special to me because it brings everyone together.
- I feel good when I do things right and follow directions carefully.
- Safety is important, and I make sure to be careful when exploring and playing.
- When someone needs a hand, I'm there to help and make things easier for them.
- I think being kind and polite to others is one of the nicest things you can do.
- Doing well and trying my best at school or in activities makes me feel proud.
- Even if something is hard, I'll keep trying because perseverance is key!

The Green Personality

- I love figuring out how things work, like puzzles, toys, or games!
- When someone tells me a fact, I like to ask "why" to understand it better.
- I get really excited when I discover something new or learn an interesting fact.
- My friends often ask me for help with homework because I enjoy sharing what I know.
- I like reading books or watching shows that teach me new and exciting things.
- Sometimes I like to have time alone to think, read, or explore my own interests.
- When I listen to stories or watch movies, I often think about how I would solve the problems or mysteries.
- In a group, I sometimes watch first so I can understand before I join in.
- I like to share interesting facts and things I've learned with my family and friends.
- When we play games, I enjoy coming up with strategies to win!
- I prefer to talk about ideas and information rather than what happened during my day.
- My curiosity leads me to ask lots of questions because I love learning new things.
- I enjoy doing activities that challenge my brain and make me think.
- Even if a task is hard, I want to try to figure it out by myself first.
- I sometimes like to imagine new inventions or explore creative ideas in my mind.

- If I believe in something, I stand firm in my opinion and explain why.
- I find joy in exploring different possibilities and trying things in various ways.
- My creativity comes alive when I am able to think freely and explore ideas.
- Finding solutions to tricky problems or challenges is super fun for me!
- I often find myself lost in thought, thinking about all sorts of ideas and possibilities.
- I appreciate honesty and truth and I try to be very straightforward with my friends.
- I love stories that take me to different worlds and let my imagination run wild.
- People often come to me when they want to know more about a topic because I love gathering information.
- I am always ready for a good debate and enjoy discussing different viewpoints.
- I think it's really important to be fair and consider all the options before making a decision.

The Orange Personality

- I'm always ready for an adventure and love trying new things!
- People say I'm fun and full of energy because I'm always moving and doing something.
- When my friends are feeling down, I try to make them laugh and cheer them up.
- I really enjoy sports, games, and anything that lets me run and play.
- I find sitting still for a long time pretty tricky because I like being active.
- When I hear music, I can't help but move and groove to the beat.
- I like to jump in and start projects, even if I haven't figured out every detail yet.
- Talking with my friends, telling stories, and sharing jokes are some of my favorite things to do.
- I'm quick to make decisions because I go with my gut feeling.
- I'd rather learn by doing things with my hands and trying them out.
- I like to make up new games and change the rules to make things even more fun!
- Sometimes I act on the spot without thinking too much, just going with the flow.
- I love surprises and unexpected fun things that pop up during my day.
- When I have a free day, I like to fill it with different and exciting activities.
- I think that learning is the most fun when it feels like playing or doing something cool.

- If something is not fun or interesting, it's really hard for me to stay focused on it.
- I'm not scared to take risks if it means having an exciting experience!
- If I see something I want, I go for it without waiting around.
- I enjoy inspiring my friends to try new things with me and explore.
- I can easily adapt to new situations and changes, it's like a fun new story!
- It's important for me to be free to make my own choices and decisions.
- I'm happiest when I can explore, be playful, and live in the moment.
- Sometimes I make quick decisions that surprise others because it just feels right.
- I feel joy when I can express myself freely and be who I want to be.
- Celebrating with friends, having parties, and being social makes my heart happy!

Chapter 12

Primary Color Quiz: Ages 10-11

In this chapter, we introduce a straightforward assessment designed specifically for 10 to 11-year-olds to pinpoint their dominant temperament. The findings are then presented in a report, highlighting key character traits and patterns, crafted with a 5th to 6th-grade reading level for easy comprehension.

Explanation

This assessment is **not** designed to be self-administered as are our adult assessments. You, as the parent or guardian, will read the instructions to your child, ask them all 24 questions, and record and tally their results.

Your child will listen and pick their favorite results. Make sure to keep it light and fun. Remind them that there are no wrong answers, only fun discoveries!

Begin by reading the instructions found below. If you choose to give your own instructions, please make sure to keep your tone light and friendly. Remind them that there are no wrong answers, only fun discoveries!

Next, read the A or B options for each question, making sure to give your child a moment to think and choose. *Don't read the colors in parenthesis, those are for your use in the scoring process.*

As they answer a question, on a spare piece of paper you can write down the four colors, Blue, Gold, Green, and Orange and then make a tally mark next to the color every time they choose that color. There is also a scoring box at the end of the assessment if you want to use it.

After the 24 questions have been answered, tally up the number of times they chose each color and record it. The highest number is their primary color. The next highest score may hint at their secondary color, but this type of AB test is not designed to measure their complete spectrum, just their primary color.

There is a summary at the end of each assessment for all four temperaments. Feel free to share that with your child. It is written at their reading level. They may also benefit from learning about the other three colors and trying to figure out the personality type of their family and friends.

Instructions

> TO BE READ BY PARENT TO CHILD

Welcome to a super fun quiz called the "Primary Color Quiz!" Are you ready to find a special color that's just like you? It might be Blue, Gold, Green, or Orange—each one is super cool in its own way! Let's dive in together and find out!

Here's how we'll play this colorful game. I'm going to read out some questions to you. Each question will have two choices—an A and a B. Listen closely to both and think about which one sounds more like you! Sometimes it might feel like both answers fit, and that's okay—just choose the one that feels extra special and a tiny bit more like you!

Now, the super important part: Be your wonderful self! There are no wrong answers here, so pick the one that really feels right in your heart, not what you think others might choose.

We're in no rush! Take a moment to think about your answer, but remember—your first feeling is usually spot-on! So no need to think too hard about it.

And guess what? We're here to have a whole bunch of fun! This isn't a test, it's a fun way to think about all the awesome things that make you, well, YOU!

Once we've gone through all the questions, we'll count up your answers together and find out which fantastic color is a lot like you!

Ready to find your color and have some fun? Let's do it!

Primary Color Quiz

	A	B
1	I enjoy being spontaneous and finding adventures. (Orange)	I love having deep talks with my friends. (Blue)
2	I'm always curious about how things work. (Green)	I love creating fun art or crafts with friends. (Blue)
3	I feel happy when everything is in order and organized. (Gold)	I enjoy exploring and understanding nature. (Green)
4	I am interested in how plants grow and survive. (Green)	I find joy in helping and taking care of my friends. (Blue)
5	I express my feelings through writing or drawing. (Blue)	I like ensuring all my work is complete and accurate. (Gold)
6	I believe in being sincere and honest with my friends. (Blue)	I enjoy trying new, exciting activities without much planning. (Orange)
7	I prefer to follow rules and respect traditions. (Gold)	I love making quick decisions and jumping into action. (Orange)
8	I like to set goals and work hard to achieve them. (Gold)	I value deep, meaningful connections with my friends. (Blue)

9	I seek thrill and excitement in the games I play. (Orange)	I enjoy learning facts and trivia about various topics. (Green)
10	I am interested in understanding different animals. (Green)	I believe it's crucial to be punctual and timely. (Gold)
11	I feel good when I am supportive and kind to others. (Blue)	I like challenging my mind with complex puzzles. (Green)
12	I find peace in reflecting on my thoughts and feelings. (Blue)	I love being energetic and lively in my actions. (Orange)
13	I feel secure when things are stable and predictable. (Gold)	I enjoy discovering why certain events happened in history. (Green)
14	I appreciate when things are systematic and orderly. (Gold)	I value sharing and listening to stories from my friends. (Blue)
15	I believe in promoting harmony and peace among friends. (Blue)	I find satisfaction in accomplishing tasks and responsibilities. (Gold)
16	I seek answers to "how" and "why" in the things around me. (Green)	I love the rush of adrenaline from playing active games. (Orange)
17	I thrive when I can move and act freely. (Orange)	I find pleasure in gathering new information and learning. (Green)

18	I love exploring different theories and ideas. (Green)	I take pride in being dependable and reliable. (Gold)
19	I cherish moments when I can express empathy and compassion. (Blue)	I feel engaged when I can solve logical problems. (Green)
20	I love forming my own theories and hypotheses. (Green)	I seek out fun and joy in every moment, being light-hearted. (Orange)
21	I like being free-spirited and going with the flow. (Orange)	I value the importance of loyalty and commitment. (Gold)
22	I believe following a structure brings success and achievement. (Gold)	I relish moments of spontaneous and unexpected joy. (Orange)
23	I express myself by being playful and animated. (Orange)	I find depth in understanding my own and others' emotions. (Blue)
24	I want to live in the moment and embrace now. (Orange)	I take comfort in routine and knowing what to expect. (Gold)

Fantastic work! We hope you enjoyed discovering more about your personality. Remember, understanding yourself is a cool journey, and you're doing amazing! Keep being curious, and enjoy all the awesome things that make you, YOU!

Scoring

Count the Blue Answers. Begin by reviewing the answers and count every instance where the color Blue was selected. Write down the total number in the Blue box below.

Repeat for Each Color. Use the same process to tally the selections for Gold, Green, and Orange. Make sure to keep track of each color's total separately to avoid any confusion.

Identifying the Dominant Color. Identify which color has the highest total number—that color is most representative of your child's personality according to the quiz.

BLUE	GOLD	GREEN	ORANGE

The Blue Personality

- I feel happiest when I can help my friends and make them smile.
- Understanding how other people feel is something that comes naturally to me.
- When someone is sad or upset, I really want to find ways to make them feel better.
- I believe it's really important to be kind and considerate to everyone I meet.
- My friends often come to me with their problems because they know I will listen.
- I tend to think a lot about how my actions will affect other people.
- Sometimes, I find myself daydreaming about exciting, imaginative worlds.
- When I read books or watch movies, I often feel deeply connected to the characters.
- Creating art, writing stories, or playing music allows me to express my feelings.
- I value deep, meaningful conversations more than just casual chats.
- It's important to me that the people around me are happy and safe.
- I often think about how I can make the world a better place, even in small ways.
- My heart feels warm and happy when I see love and peace around me.
- I'm not afraid to stand up for my friends and what I believe is right.
- When I make decisions, I always consider my feelings and values.

- It's essential for me to have harmony in my group and avoid fights or arguments.
- I love animals because they also have feelings and love to give.
- When someone is being treated unfairly, it makes me upset and I want to help.
- I often find beauty in things and places where others might not notice it.
- I prefer to focus on the positive side of life and keep hope alive in tough times.
- Friendships and relationships are like treasures to me, and I care for them deeply.
- I try to find solutions that make everyone happy and keep things fair.
- It's hard for me to hide my emotions because I wear my heart on my sleeve.
- I believe that everyone has goodness inside them, and I try to see that.
- My dreams and ideals guide me, and I believe in chasing after them with all my heart.

The Gold Personality

- I like having a plan for what I'm going to do each day.
- When I make a promise, I do everything I can to keep it.
- I feel good when things are organized and in their proper places.
- Being on time is important to me because it shows respect for others.
- I prefer following rules and expect others to do the same.
- It's really satisfying for me to finish all my homework and chores.
- I enjoy being in groups and teams where everyone does their part.
- My friends know they can count on me because I'm reliable.
- When things change suddenly, it can make me feel uneasy.
- I respect people who are responsible and trustworthy.
- I like to show appreciation to people by doing nice things for them.
- It makes me feel proud when I am recognized for my hard work.
- My family and traditions are very special and important to me.
- I often find myself helping others in practical, useful ways.
- It's vital for me to have clear instructions so I know what to do.

- I believe that if something works well, it's best to stick with it.
- If I'm in charge of a project, I'll make sure everything is arranged and structured.
- I keep track of important dates, like friends' birthdays, so I can celebrate them.
- Being prepared and having everything I need makes me feel secure.
- I value authority figures and listen carefully to their advice.
- It's crucial for me to make choices that are safe and sensible.
- I like to make lists to ensure I don't forget anything important.
- I enjoy activities more when they're scheduled and not spontaneous.
- In a group, I usually take on the role of organizing and coordinating.
- I believe that doing things correctly is more important than doing them quickly.

The Green Personality

- I love to explore new ideas and think about future possibilities.
- When I learn something, I like to dive deep and understand it fully.
- I get really excited when I solve a tricky problem all by myself.
- It's fun for me to imagine and invent things that don't exist yet.
- I often wonder how things work and sometimes take them apart to see.
- I believe that there's always a logical answer to every question.
- I enjoy reading books or watching shows that make me think hard.
- When I argue, it's not to be mean, but to understand things better.
- I like to have debates with my friends about various topics.
- I get bored if I have to do things that are too easy or repetitive.
- I'm usually the one who comes up with new games or activities.
- Even if my ideas seem odd to others, I trust my own logic.
- It's important for me to make decisions based on facts, not feelings.
- Sometimes I prefer spending time on my interests instead of socializing.
- I don't mind being different or unique compared to others.

- When I'm curious about something, I'll research it until I understand it.
- I get frustrated when people don't listen to logical explanations.
- I appreciate teachers or adults who respect my unusual ideas.
- Being independent and self-reliant is something I take pride in.
- I may not show my emotions much, but I deeply care about my close ones.
- I often envision how I could improve things or make them more efficient.
- I am determined to achieve my goals, even if they seem tough.
- My mind is always busy with thoughts, even when I'm not talking.
- I value honesty and prefer people to be straightforward with me.
- I'd rather fail while trying something challenging than succeed in something easy.

The Orange Personality

- I really enjoy being active and having lots of fun moving around.
- Trying out new and exciting things is one of my favorite things to do.
- My friends and I love to go on adventures together.
- When I see a problem, I like to solve it right away and not wait.
- Sometimes, I act on my feelings without spending too much time thinking.
- I believe that life should be full of joy and exciting experiences.
- When I want something, I find creative ways to make it happen.
- Playing games with lots of action and excitement is super fun for me.
- I learn best when I can touch, build, and interact with things.
- I often lighten the mood by making my friends and family laugh.
- I don't like to plan too much; I prefer to go with the flow.
- My day is way better when it's filled with lots of different activities.
- I like to live in the moment and not worry too much about the future.
- Being free to do what I want is really important to me.
- I'm pretty good at adapting to whatever situation I find myself in.
- Sometimes, I take risks just for the thrill of it.

- I usually choose to do things the fast and fun way, not the slow and safe way.
- If a task seems boring, I'll find a way to make it interesting.
- I can quickly think on my feet and make decisions in the moment.
- My friends count on me to come up with spontaneous plans.
- I communicate best when I can express myself freely and openly.
- I find practical and hands-on solutions to problems I face.
- Sometimes, I'd rather act first and deal with the consequences later.
- When it comes to teamwork, I shine in dynamic and lively environments.
- I celebrate my successes and don't dwell too long on my mistakes.

Chapter 13

Primary Color Quiz: Ages 12-13

In this chapter, we introduce a straightforward assessment designed specifically for 12 to 13-year-olds to pinpoint their dominant temperament. The findings are then presented in a report, highlighting key character traits and patterns, crafted with a 7th to 8th-grade reading level for easy comprehension.

Explanation

This assessment is **not** designed to be self-administered as are our adult assessments. You, as the parent or guardian, will read the instructions to your child, ask them all 24 questions, and record and tally their results.

Your child will listen and pick their favorite results. Make sure to keep it light and fun. Remind them that there are no wrong answers, only fun discoveries!

Begin by reading the instructions found below. If you choose to give your own instructions, please make sure to keep your tone light and friendly. Remind them that there are no wrong answers, only fun discoveries!

Next, read the A or B options for each question, making sure to give your child a moment to think and choose. *Don't read the colors in parenthesis, those are for your use in the scoring process.*

As they answer a question, on a spare piece of paper you can write down the four colors, Blue, Gold, Green, and Orange and then make a tally mark next to the color every time they choose that color. There is also a scoring box at the end of the assessment if you want to use it.

After the 24 questions have been answered, tally up the number of times they chose each color and record it. The highest number is their primary color. The next highest score may hint at their secondary color, but this type of AB test is not designed to measure their complete spectrum, just their primary color.

There is a summary at the end of each assessment for all four temperaments. Feel free to share that with your child. It is written at their reading level. They may also benefit from learning about the other three colors and trying to figure out the personality type of their family and friends.

Instructions

> TO BE READ BY PARENT TO CHILD

Welcome to the "Primary Color Quiz" personality test! Are you curious to find out which color best represents your unique personality? Whether it's Blue, Gold, Green, or Orange, each color symbolizes different cool traits and characteristics. Let's embark on this journey together and unveil your color!

Here's the rundown: I'm going to read out some questions, and for each one, you'll hear two options—A and B. Tune in to each option and ponder which one aligns more with who you are! If you feel both answers could suit you, that's totally fine—just choose the one that nudges closer to your true self.

Key note: Be real! There's no such thing as a wrong answer here, so choose the option that genuinely feels like "you," not what you think others might expect or want.

Feel free to take a moment to reflect on your answer, but remember that sometimes, your initial gut feeling is right on the mark!

Let's not forget: This is all about enjoying the process! It's not a test but a fun and enlightening exploration into understanding all the fabulous qualities that make you, YOU!

After we've explored all the questions, we'll tally up your responses and unveil which color mirrors your personality! Are you ready to discover your color and enjoy the ride? Let's dive in!

Primary Color Quiz

	A	B
1	I find peace in creating art. (Blue)	I always keep my workspace organized. (Gold)
2	I'm always excited to try new adventures. (Orange)	I believe in sticking to a routine. (Gold)
3	I enjoy acting in school plays. (Orange)	I love exploring how technology works. (Green)
4	I feel proud when I am punctual. (Gold)	I like reading about scientific discoveries. (Green)
5	I value deep conversations with my friends. (Blue)	I am happiest when being active and moving. (Orange)
6	I respect the rules at school. (Gold)	I seek thrilling experiences. (Orange)
7	I enjoy solving challenging puzzles. (Green)	I am drawn to listening and helping others. (Blue)
8	I like experimenting with new ideas. (Green)	I find joy in expressing myself through writing. (Blue)
9	I always question how things work. (Green)	I feel accomplished after completing a task. (Gold)

Insightful Parenting 1 ■ 225

10	I appreciate the harmony in music. (Blue)	I am fascinated by inventions and innovations. (Green)
11	I often get lost in thought about the universe. (Green)	I spontaneously start fun projects. (Orange)
12	I love exploring unknown places. (Orange)	I find satisfaction in acquiring knowledge. (Green)
13	I prioritize living in the moment. (Orange)	I believe in being responsible and prepared. (Gold)
14	I get excited about learning new facts. (Green)	I embrace challenges with open arms. (Orange)
15	I enjoy exploring theoretical concepts. (Green)	I appreciate having clear instructions. (Gold)
16	I am moved by the stories of others. (Blue)	I am always up for a spontaneous road trip. (Orange)
17	I value traditions and heritage. (Gold)	I believe in the importance of empathy. (Blue)
18	I prioritize accomplishing my goals. (Gold)	I cherish my time connecting with nature. (Blue)

19	I find excitement in unexpected surprises. (Orange)	I seek deep and meaningful friendships. (Blue)
20	I adhere to the systems that have been set. (Gold)	I am curious about discovering new possibilities. (Green)
21	I enjoy arranging and coordinating events. (Gold)	I believe in following my heart's desires. (Orange)
22	I feel alive when immersed in a good book. (Blue)	I find security in proven methods. (Gold)
23	I prefer activities that pump up my adrenaline. (Orange)	I express myself through various art forms. (Blue)
24	I treasure the moments of calm and solitude. (Blue)	I get inspired by the wonders of the outer space. (Green)

Well done on finishing the assessment! Understanding more about yourself can be exciting and helpful. Keep exploring your interests and embracing your uniqueness. Remember, you're growing up, and there's so much more to learn and discover about yourself!

Scoring

Count the Blue Answers. Begin by reviewing the answers and count every instance where the color Blue was selected. Write down the total number in the Blue box below.

Repeat for Each Color. Use the same process to tally the selections for Gold, Green, and Orange. Make sure to keep track of each color's total separately to avoid any confusion.

Identifying the Dominant Color. Identify which color has the highest total number—that color is most representative of your child's personality according to the quiz.

BLUE	GOLD	GREEN	ORANGE

The Blue Personality

- I often find myself being drawn to and deeply moved by various forms of art and expression.
- The feelings and well-being of the people around me really matter to me, and I'm always ready to lend a listening ear.
- I seek deep, meaningful connections with my friends and family and cherish every moment with them.
- Often, I daydream about different possibilities, future events, and exciting adventures that await.
- My emotions run deep, and I experience joy and sadness quite intensely.
- I am always on the lookout for ways to make positive changes in the lives of others.
- People often come to me for comfort and advice because they know I understand and validate their feelings.
- I believe in the power of positive thinking and always try to see the good in every situation.
- Honesty and authenticity in relationships are incredibly important to me; I value genuine connections.
- I seek harmony and tend to avoid conflicts, preferring peaceful solutions whenever possible.
- It's natural for me to empathize with others, putting myself in their shoes to understand their emotions and perspectives.
- Injustice and unfairness really bother me, and I strive to stand up for what's right.
- I deeply appreciate when people express their gratitude or acknowledge me in a heartfelt way.

- I value personal growth and always seek ways to better understand myself and others.
- When it comes to decision-making, I always consider how the outcome will affect the people involved.
- My intuition often guides me, helping me to read between the lines and perceive things that might not be obvious.
- Encouraging and supporting others in their endeavors brings me a lot of joy and fulfillment.
- I dream of a world where everyone is kind, compassionate, and understands one another.
- I'm not just looking for friendships; I seek soulful connections and bonds that last a lifetime.
- My creativity often finds its way into my activities, projects, and solutions to problems.
- When someone is feeling down, I feel a strong desire to uplift them and brighten their day.
- I seek and cherish moments of deep, reflective solitude where I can explore my thoughts and feelings.
- I strive to be a beacon of positivity and inspiration for those around me.
- Sincerity is key in my interactions, and I deeply appreciate genuine gestures and words.
- I find metaphors and symbols to be deeply moving, often seeing deeper meanings in various aspects of life.

The Gold Personality

- I find comfort and satisfaction in creating and following routines in my daily life.
- When I make a commitment, sticking to it and being reliable is super important to me.
- Organizing events, tasks, or activities is something I naturally lean into and enjoy.
- I usually prioritize my duties and responsibilities before fun and relaxation.
- Being punctual and respecting others' time is a principle that I live by.
- I value traditions and often enjoy celebrating holidays and occasions in a time-honored way.
- When working in a group, I am usually the one who helps keep everything on track.
- It's important for me to be well-prepared for any situation, so I plan meticulously.
- I believe in respecting authority and listening to the wisdom of those more experienced than me.
- My friends and family know me as someone they can depend on, no matter what.
- When I say I'll do something, I make sure it gets done and to the best of my ability.
- I am often cautious and think things through before making decisions or taking actions.
- I feel a strong sense of duty to help others and contribute to my community.
- My decisions are usually guided by practicality and what has proven to work in the past.
- I like knowing what to expect, so surprises or last-minute changes can be a bit unsettling for me.

- My moral compass and doing what's right is something that I hold dear.
- Consistency is key for me, and I appreciate when life and people are predictable and stable.
- I often take on leadership roles by ensuring that things run smoothly and are well-organized.
- For me, respecting and following the rules is not just necessary, it's the right thing to do.
- I find pleasure in being of service to others and ensuring they can count on me.
- A well-structured plan and clear instructions make me feel confident and secure.
- My friendships are often long-lasting because loyalty is really significant to me.
- Making a positive impact on my community or group is something I aspire to do.
- Being recognized for my hard work and reliability is both motivating and gratifying.
- I tend to be careful and thoughtful, especially when it comes to making decisions that affect others.

The Green Personality

- I find joy in exploring and understanding complex ideas and theories.
- When I solve a challenging problem or puzzle, I feel truly invigorated.
- Others often admire my strategic and forward-thinking mind.
- It's vital for me to be competent and knowledgeable in the subjects that interest me.
- I am on a continuous quest for knowledge and always keen to learn more.
- Sometimes, I prefer exploring the world of ideas to socializing with people.
- I value logic and reason, making decisions based on facts and data.
- Efficiency is crucial to me; I'm always looking for the best way to achieve my goals.
- When I am determined to achieve something, it's hard to sway my focus.
- I strive to be innovative and often think outside of the conventional box.
- Sometimes I get so absorbed in my thoughts or projects that I lose track of time.
- I respect people who present their arguments with logic and credible evidence.
- My dreams often involve creating or inventing something impactful and significant.
- I usually prefer to communicate through precise and clear language.
- Complex challenges are fascinating and I love dissecting them to understand how they work.

- I appreciate honest and constructive criticism as it helps me grow and improve.
- Often, I prefer working alone because it allows me to fully engage with my thoughts.
- I may seem reserved, but my inner world is bursting with innovative and creative ideas.
- My independence is crucial to me; I desire the freedom to explore my own paths and ideas.
- I naturally gravitate toward leadership roles where I can implement my visions.
- When faced with a problem, I usually start by analyzing all possible solutions.
- I respect competence and expertise and seek to be an expert in my areas of interest.
- Continuous self-improvement and learning are vital parts of my life.
- I enjoy debating ideas and concepts, testing their validity through discussion.
- My curiosity often leads me to explore unconventional and novel approaches.

The Orange Personality

- I'm the person who is always up for a spontaneous adventure and trying new things.
- Living in the present moment and soaking up the fun is really my style.
- I thrive in situations where I can be hands-on and actively involved.
- My friends often look to me when they want to lighten the mood or need a good laugh.
- Quick decision-making is one of my strengths, especially in fast-paced situations.
- I cherish my freedom and love having the ability to choose my own path.
- When it comes to rules, sometimes I bend them a bit to make life more exciting.
- I tend to be pretty adaptable, easily rolling with the punches life throws at me.
- People often admire my practical and direct approach to solving problems.
- I enjoy being playful and often bring an element of surprise to my group of friends.
- Living for today and seeking joyful experiences is crucial for me.
- I can be quite persuasive when I'm passionate about something and want others to join in.
- Sometimes I act on a whim, going with my gut feeling in that moment.
- I'm not afraid to take risks if it means having a memorable experience.
- Challenges and competitions spark my energy, especially if they're physical.

- I express myself best when I'm being straightforward and genuine.
- The idea of a routine tends to bore me; I prefer a varied and dynamic day.
- My learning style often involves interacting with and manipulating my surroundings.
- I find that my straightforward, to-the-point communication style works best for me.
- Often, I'm the one who rallies my friends together for impromptu plans or outings.
- I appreciate tangible rewards and recognition for my efforts and achievements.
- Navigating through chaos and changing circumstances comes naturally to me.
- I believe that life should be lived fully, with a healthy dose of fun and excitement.
- My energy often uplifts and motivates the people around me.
- While I enjoy being social and lively, I also value my freedom and autonomy.

Chapter 14

Primary Color Quiz: Ages 14-15

In this chapter, we introduce a straightforward assessment designed specifically for 14 to 15-year-olds to pinpoint their dominant temperament. The findings are then presented in a report, highlighting key character traits and patterns, crafted with an age-appropriate reading level for easy comprehension.

Explanation

This assessment is **not** designed to be self-administered as are our adult assessments. You, as the parent or guardian, will read the instructions to your teenager, ask them all 24 questions, and record and tally their results.

Your teenager will listen and pick their favorite results. Make sure to keep it light and fun. Remind them that there are no wrong answers, only fun discoveries!

Begin by reading the instructions found below. If you choose to give your own instructions, please make sure to keep your tone light and friendly. Remind them that there are no wrong answers, only fun discoveries!

Next, read the A or B options for each question, making sure to give your teenager a moment to think and choose. *Don't read the colors in parenthesis, those are for your use in the scoring process.*

As they answer a question, on a spare piece of paper you can write down the four colors, Blue, Gold, Green, and Orange and then make a tally mark next to the color every time they choose that color. There is also a scoring box at the end of the assessment if you want to use it.

After the 24 questions have been answered, tally up the number of times they chose each color and record it. The highest number is their primary color. The next highest score may hint at their secondary color, but this type of AB test is not designed to measure their complete spectrum, just their primary color.

There is a summary at the end of each assessment for all four temperaments. Feel free to share that with your teenager. It is written at their reading level. They may also benefit from learning about the other three colors and trying to figure out the personality type of their family and friends.

Instructions

> TO BE READ BY PARENT TO TEENAGER

Welcome to the "Primary Color Quiz," a personality test crafted to delve into what makes you, uniquely you! Intrigued to unearth which color—Blue, Gold, Green, or Orange—resonates with your personality? Each color symbolizes distinct and equally fascinating characteristics. So, let's navigate this explorative journey together and unveil your representative color!

Here's the drill: I'll read out some questions, each providing two options—A and B. Your task? Reflect on each one and decide which resonates more with your personality! It might feel like both are fitting at times, and that's completely okay. Just opt for the one that feels a smidge more "you."

Crucial point to remember: Be authentically you! No wrong answers here; your selection should resonate with who you genuinely are, devoid of external expectations.

Take a moment, but don't stress over your decision. Often, your initial instinct is incredibly insightful, so trust it.

This isn't a test, but a journey to appreciate and explore your marvelous individuality! Once we've perused all the questions, we'll add up your choices and disclose which color parallels your personality!

Are you geared up to delve into this explorative journey and unveil your color? Let's get started!

Primary Color Quiz

	A	B
1	I feel happiest when I'm helping others. (Blue)	I like figuring out problems logically. (Green)
2	I enjoy comforting friends when they're sad. (Blue)	I find joy in organizing and planning events. (Gold)
3	I value traditions and family gatherings. (Gold)	I'm interested in learning new scientific facts. (Green)
4	I like to explore and understand new technologies. (Green)	I believe understanding emotions is crucial. (Blue)
5	I'm thrilled by spontaneous adventures. (Orange)	I enjoy conducting experiments to learn. (Green)
6	I get excited about mastering new mathematical concepts. (Green)	I value deep and meaningful conversations. (Blue)
7	I appreciate when things are systematic and orderly. (Green)	I find happiness in living in the moment. (Orange)
8	I'm drawn to learning about various plants and animals. (Green)	I believe it's important to respect rules and order. (Gold)

9	I find satisfaction in completing tasks accurately. (Gold)	I love exploring new places without a plan. (Orange)
10	I enjoy getting my energy from lively and energetic environments. (Orange)	I feel it's essential to be empathetic towards others. (Blue)
11	I am fulfilled when I follow my daily routines. (Gold)	I find excitement in trying something new and unpredictable. (Orange)
12	I value in-depth research before forming an opinion. (Green)	I believe maintaining a schedule is crucial for success. (Gold)
13	I think promoting a harmonious environment is vital. (Blue)	I enjoy discussing theoretical and abstract concepts. (Green)
14	I take pride in being punctual and disciplined. (Gold)	I prioritize developing strong bonds with friends. (Blue)
15	I value reliability and consistency in life. (Gold)	I believe in being considerate and caring towards everyone. (Blue)
16	I value emotional connections with people. (Blue)	I believe in preserving and valuing historical facts and stories. (Gold)
17	I cherish freedom and the ability to make instant decisions. (Orange)	I find security in having a clear set of rules. (Gold)

18	I find joy in providing support and encouragement to friends. (Blue)	I enjoy engaging in thrilling physical activities. (Orange)
19	I value living a dynamic and diverse life. (Orange)	I find comfort in stability and a predictable environment. (Gold)
20	I like to explore ideas and innovations critically. (Green)	I enjoy expressing myself through creative and artistic pursuits. (Orange)
21	I seek out fun and excitement regularly. (Orange)	I enjoy engaging in intellectually stimulating puzzles and games. (Green)
22	I feel it's important to be compassionate and kind-hearted. (Blue)	I thrive in environments where I can be active and energetic. (Orange)
23	I feel content when everything is in order and organized. (Gold)	I enjoy exploring new scientific ideas and innovations. (Green)
24	I believe in taking risks and embracing challenges. (Orange)	I find fulfillment in helping and guiding others. (Blue)

Congratulations on completing the assessment! We hope it provided you with some interesting insights. As you continue to grow and learn, remember that embracing your uniqueness is what makes you stand out. Stay true to yourself and enjoy the journey of self-discovery!

Scoring

Count the Blue Answers. Begin by reviewing the answers and count every instance where the color Blue was selected. Write down the total number in the Blue box below.

Repeat for Each Color. Use the same process to tally the selections for Gold, Green, and Orange. Make sure to keep track of each color's total separately to avoid any confusion.

Identifying the Dominant Color. Identify which color has the highest total number—that color is most representative of your child's personality according to the quiz.

BLUE	GOLD	GREEN	ORANGE

The Blue Personality

- I seamlessly find myself intuitively enveloping the emotional climates within various situations, keenly sensing and absorbing the underlying vibes that permeate a room.

- Authenticity within my relationships transcends importance; it stands as a staunch, non-negotiable principle, compelling me to forge only real and utterly unfiltered connections.

- I'm not only an advocate but a steadfast believer in the transformative, life-altering power of positive affirmations, and consistently strive to be a beacon of optimism.

- Exhibiting understanding and showcasing compassion towards others is not merely a conscious choice; it's intrinsically woven into the very fabric of my being.

- I am frequently embarking on introspective journeys into my rich, multifaceted internal world, exploring my thoughts and feelings with an endless, fervent curiosity.

- My intrinsic value for empathy invariably transforms into active advocacy; the sight of injustice propels me into action, as standing idle is an unthinkable option.

- Artistic expressions deeply resonate within me, compelling me to gravitate towards various vibrant and emotionally-rich forms of creative outputs and mediums.

- Friendships, in my world, transgress being mere social connections; they materialize as profoundly cherished, soulful bonds that I hold close to my heart.

- I perpetually dive into the expansive depths of my imagination, permitting myself the freedom to envision a myriad of possibilities and hypothetical scenarios.
- I habitually perceive the nuanced and often unspoken emotions in others, delicately picking up on subtle, emotional cues that might elude others.
- My heart not only influences but decidedly guides my decisions, particularly when the emotional and physical well-being of others hangs in the balance.
- I find that the emotional experiences of those surrounding me permeate my own emotional state, invariably prompting a compassionate and heartfelt response.
- Bringing joy and providing a supportive, nurturing space for others to be their authentic selves is not just fulfilling but a source of deep, resonant joy.
- A genuine "thank you" or authentic acknowledgment not only warms my heart but also validates my efforts, making every gesture feel profoundly worthwhile.
- I am unceasingly on a path toward evolution, embracing personal growth as an enduring, ever-present element of my existential journey.
- My intuition serves as more than a guide; it gently whispers deeper, often unarticulated truths and reveals unspoken realities, which I frequently find astonishingly accurate.
- I find my optimal functioning within harmonious environments, perpetually striving to establish and maintain a tranquil peace in all group dynamics.
- Confronted with problems, I don't just seek solutions but approach them with a boundless creativity, exploring innovative, out-of-the-box methods to resolve issues effectively.

- Being a source of inspiration and motivation for others is more than joyful; it resonates as a calling, an intrinsic part of my purpose.
- Craving depth in conversations and interactions is pivotal to me, as I continually seek connections that surpass the superficial and delve beneath the surface.
- My fervent desire to make a positive impact transcends actions, aiming to instigate a more expansive wave of kindness, empathy, and understanding across my environment.
- In moments of solitude, I find abundant company within my thoughts, traversing through various facets of my feelings and complex ideologies.
- I perpetually search for symbolic meanings within events and circumstances, holding a firm belief that deeper, more profound understandings linger beneath the observable surface.
- I aspire beyond seeking peace; I aim to serve as a catalyst, actively creating and nurturing harmonious environments wherever my path takes me.
- Emotional intelligence, for me, transcends being a skill; it acts as a nuanced lens through which I perceive, interpret, and navigate my interpersonal relationships.

The Gold Personality

- I pride myself on being someone my friends and family can always count on, especially when reliability is key.

- For me, maintaining order isn't just practical; it's a pathway to efficiency and clarity in both thoughts and actions.

- I genuinely find joy in creating lists and schedules because they bring a sense of predictability and control to my day.

- Traditions are more to me than recurrent events; they are symbolic, connecting me to my roots and providing a sense of continuity.

- Being punctual isn't merely about time management; it reflects my respect for other people's time and commitments.

- My moral compass doesn't waver amidst dilemmas; I adhere to my values, ensuring they guide my decisions and actions.

- When I commit to a task, I immerse myself wholeheartedly, ensuring each detail is addressed with diligence.

- My friendships aren't just social connections; they're bonds forged with loyalty and a silent promise of steadfast support.

- In a team, I often find myself naturally aligning with a leadership role, steering the group towards our goals with structured plans.

- I value stability, not just in my surroundings but in relationships, thriving in environments where consistency is present.

- When challenges arise, I confront them with a structured approach, dissecting problems into manageable parts.
- I find satisfaction in helping others, particularly through acts of service that bring order and ease to their lives.
- Efficiency isn't just about getting things done; it's a principle that I integrate into every facet of my life.
- My respect for authority stems from a belief in structure and the notion that it maintains societal balance.
- I tend to seek logical solutions to problems, ensuring that my decisions are informed and rational.
- Commitment to me is not bound to words; it's reflected through persistent actions and unwavering loyalty.
- Respect for me is bilateral; I give it generously and anticipate it in return, viewing it as a fundamental aspect of relationships.
- My goals aren't mere destinations; they're drivers that shape my actions and decisions daily.
- In conflicts, I prioritize resolution and stability, ensuring harmony is restored through compromise and understanding.
- A clean and organized space doesn't just look good; it clears my mind and enhances my focus and productivity.
- I naturally gravitate towards roles where I can foster unity and cooperative functioning within a group.
- I tend to internalize societal expectations, striving to align my actions and achievements with recognized standards.

- Fairness is paramount to me, and I strive to ensure that my actions and decisions exemplify impartiality and justice.
- My sense of duty often propels me into positions of responsibility, where I manage tasks with meticulous care.
- I approach change cautiously, ensuring adaptations do not compromise the foundation of my values and stability.

The Green Personality

- I find myself constantly intrigued by puzzles and problems, seeing them as challenges to be conquered with logic.
- My curiosity isn't confined; it's an insatiable quest for knowledge, spanning various topics and domains.
- Often, I discover myself deeply absorbed in thoughts, exploring various scenarios and solutions within my mind.
- Being competent isn't just a trait for me; it's a commitment to ensuring that every task I undertake is executed proficiently.
- Autonomy is pivotal to me, granting me the freedom to explore, understand, and create without constraints.
- While I value relationships, I tend to gravitate towards people who share a similar thirst for knowledge and discovery.
- I don't merely accept facts; I scrutinize them, ensuring they endure the rigors of my logical examination.
- My aspirations often traverse the conventional, steering towards the innovative and the ingeniously challenging.
- I revel in complexity, viewing it not as a hurdle, but as a fascinating tapestry of interconnected issues to unravel.
- Strategy isn't just a plan for me; it's an art, weaving together foresight, insight, and calculated risks.
- I find fulfillment in dissecting theories, peering into their depths, and reconstructing them with added value.

- Efficiency to me isn't just speed; it's about optimizing every aspect of a process to attain the maximum output with minimum input.
- I derive satisfaction from producing quality work, ensuring it not only meets but surpasses established standards.
- In debates, I don't just participate; I strategize, ensuring my arguments are logically sound and empirically substantiated.
- I instinctively seek patterns and correlations, eager to comprehend the underlying mechanisms of phenomena
- Visionary isn't just a descriptor for me; it's an integral part of who I am, always envisioning possibilities and futures.
- I embrace change when it's backed by rationality, ensuring progress and evolution.
- My decision-making isn't impulsive; it's methodically thought-out, considering all plausible outcomes.
- I immerse myself in innovation, constantly seeking to invent or enhance in every project I undertake.
- I typically seek clarity in communication, ensuring that messages are precise, concise, and devoid of ambiguity.
- For me, leadership isn't about authority; it's about guiding a team strategically towards collective and innovative success.
- I'm not swayed by emotions in debates; instead, I anchor my responses in facts and logical consistency.
- Learning for me isn't confined to institutions; it's a perpetual endeavor, absorbing knowledge from various sources.

- I am perpetually forward-looking, contemplating the implications of actions and decisions in a broader temporal context.
- I am not resistant to critiques; rather, I welcome them when they're constructive and facilitate improvement.

The Orange Personality

- I'm an unwavering bundle of vibrant energy, perpetually prepared to dive into my subsequent adventure or confront a new, exhilarating challenge with zest.

- Flexibility defines not only a trait but also intricately weaves into my lifestyle, as I navigate through life's unpredictable ebbs and flows with effortless adaptability and a loose grip on expectations.

- My inherent spontaneity functions as my distinct trademark, enabling me to embrace opportunities impromptu, without being restrained by overly detailed or stringent plans.

- My decisions pivot primarily on the thrill and appeal of the immediate moment, being fueled and propelled by whatever specifically ignites my excitement and interest right then and there.

- Although I am certainly capable of forming profound connections, my focus is squarely on immersing myself fully in the absorbing present, cherishing every exhilarating and fleeting second.

- To me, life emerges as a vivaciously vibrant tapestry, densely woven with myriad experiences that beckon to be both passionately explored and richly savored.

- I not only thrive but also find my equilibrium in engaging with the tangible and the palpable, seeking out experiences that I can actively see, touch, and profoundly feel.

- My style of communication is unswervingly straightforward and genuine, completely devoid of underlying complexity or potentially hidden agendas and intentions.

- Risks, in my perspective, are not entities to be feared but enthusiastically embraced, as they carve out pathways to adventures that make my heart race and enable new, exciting discoveries.
- I extract my vitality from energetically interacting with a diverse array of people, delving into varied cultures, and wholeheartedly immersing myself in a plethora of different environments.
- My view of learning is not rigidly confined to textbooks but expansively extends into the realm of practical experiences and hands-on, active involvement.
- A resistance to being constricted by routines characterizes me, as I perpetually seek both variety and spontaneity in all my daily endeavors and activities.
- My creativity frequently bursts forth in the shape of practical, applicable solutions and innovative, on-the-fly problem-solving approaches.
- Whenever I encounter rules, my indomitable spirit instinctively seeks to explore and push against boundaries, rigorously testing the limits of possibilities.
- Preserving the freedom to choose, act, and live in alignment with my immediate impulses is not just important but absolutely paramount to my happiness and intrinsic sense of self.
- My friendships are thoroughly infused with lively fun, numerous activities, and shared, adventurous experiences, fortifying bonds through collective, joyous experiences.
- I find pure, unadulterated joy in life's physicality, engaging in activities that permit me to move, express, and experience in a viscerally palpable manner.

- My resilience is robust, allowing me to rebound from setbacks with a persistently optimistic spirit and a preparedness to handle whatever comes next with grace.
- Far from being mere distractions, impulses serve as my guideposts, unerringly leading me toward experiences that are thoroughly exhilarating and heart-pounding.
- I am unabashedly and unapologetically myself, consistently unfiltered and genuine, sharing my thoughts and feelings without a moment's hesitation or doubt.
- In my view, leadership doesn't hinge on control but focuses on energetically rallying people toward collective action, which is infused with vibrant energy and enjoyment.
- My celebrations are firmly rooted in the present moment, finding boundless joy in the now without becoming entangled in the webs of past regrets or potential future worries.
- Practicality stands key in my actions and decisions, ensuring that ideas and plans are not only viable but also immediately applicable and effortlessly executable.
- I am a doer, decisively preferring to take spirited action and make things happen rather than becoming bogged down in extensive contemplation or meticulous planning.
- Regarding challenges, I confront them directly, transforming obstacles into exciting, engaging hurdles to be overcome on life's endlessly thrilling and vibrant journey.

Chapter 15

Primary Color Quiz: Ages 16-17

In this chapter, we introduce a straightforward assessment designed specifically for 16 to 17-year-olds to pinpoint their dominant temperament. The findings are then presented in a report, highlighting key character traits and patterns, crafted with an age-appropriate reading level for easy comprehension.

Explanation

This assessment is **not** designed to be self-administered as are our adult assessments. You, as the parent or guardian, will read the instructions to your teenager, ask them all 24 questions, and record and tally their results.

Your teenager will listen and pick their favorite results. Make sure to keep it light and fun. Remind them that there are no wrong answers, only fun discoveries!

Begin by reading the instructions found below. If you choose to give your own instructions, please make sure to keep your tone light and friendly. Remind them that there are no wrong answers, only fun discoveries!

Next, read the A or B options for each question, making sure to give your teenager a moment to think and choose. *Don't read the colors in parenthesis, those are for your use in the scoring process.*

As they answer a question, on a spare piece of paper you can write down the four colors, Blue, Gold, Green, and Orange and then make a tally mark next to the color every time they choose that color. There is also a scoring box at the end of the assessment if you want to use it.

After the 24 questions have been answered, tally up the number of times they chose each color and record it. The highest number is their primary color. The next highest score may hint at their secondary color, but this type of AB test is not designed to measure their complete spectrum, just their primary color.

There is a summary at the end of each assessment for all four temperaments. Feel free to share that with your teenager. It is written at their reading level. They may also benefit from learning about the other three colors and trying to figure out the personality type of their family and friends.

Instructions

> TO BE READ BY PARENT TO TEENAGER

Welcome to the "Primary Color Quiz" personality assessment. This isn't your typical quiz; it's a chance to explore aspects of your personality in a unique and insightful way. Are you ready to see which color—Blue, Gold, Green, or Orange—mirrors your personality traits most accurately?

Here's how it's going to work: I'll read out some statements, and each will have two options, A and B. Take a moment to contemplate which one feels more authentic to your experiences and characteristics. There may be times when both seem applicable, but try to select the one that resonates with you the most.

It's crucial to approach this with genuine self-honesty. There's no right or wrong here, only what's true for you, not influenced by external perceptions or expectations.

No need to overthink your responses—often, initial instincts are quite revealing. Trust yours.

Remember, this isn't a test, but a self-exploration exercise. After going through all the questions, we'll tally your responses and reveal which color closely aligns with your personality.

Ready to embark on this insightful journey and discover your color? Let's get started.

Primary Color Quiz

	A	B
1	I appreciate a well-structured and planned life. (Gold)	I am happiest when acting spontaneously and trying new things. (Orange)
2	I prefer a free-spirited and flexible lifestyle, where I can be impulsive. (Orange)	I value punctuality and always strive to be on time. (Gold)
3	I find satisfaction in following routines and schedules. (Gold)	I believe life is best lived in the moment, even without a plan. (Orange)
4	I enjoy being lively, energetic, and possibly the life of the party. (Orange)	I find enjoyment in solving problems and understanding complex systems. (Green)
5	I value knowledge and constantly seek to understand more about the world. (Green)	I find comfort and security in traditions and established methods. (Gold)
6	I believe in trying everything at least once for the sheer thrill of it. (Orange)	I value depth in relationships and seek authentic connections with others. (Blue)

Insightful Parenting 1 ■ 261

7	I have a natural inclination toward organizing and coordinating events. (Gold)	I seek to comprehend the underlying principles of how things work. (Green)
8	I believe rules and structure are vital for a functioning community. (Gold)	I think empathy and understanding are key to harmonious interactions. (Blue)
9	I prioritize emotional intelligence and understanding others' feelings. (Blue)	I emphasize logical thinking and objective analysis. (Green)
10	I enjoy contemplating hypothetical scenarios and exploring abstract concepts. (Green)	I believe nurturing and safeguarding emotional well-being is crucial. (Blue)
11	I seek emotional depth and meaningful interactions in friendships. (Blue)	I love engaging in high-energy activities and lively interactions. (Orange)
12	I'm drawn to action, enthusiasm, and spontaneous adventures. (Orange)	I prioritize harmony and strive to resolve conflicts empathetically. (Blue)
13	I value intellectual exploration and delving into conceptual ideas. (Green)	I appreciate a pragmatic approach and realistic solutions. (Gold)

14	I find joy in exploring theories and pondering future possibilities. (Green)	I value sincere expressions of sentiment and forming close bonds. (Blue)
15	I find fulfillment in aiding and emotionally supporting others. (Blue)	I derive satisfaction from logical analysis and systematic understanding. (Green)
16	I enjoy dedicating time to thoughtful reflection and analytical thinking. (Green)	I find excitement in taking immediate action and diving into experiences. (Orange)
17	I believe taking time to listen and understand others' feelings is essential. (Blue)	I think embracing change and adventurous endeavors is vital. (Orange)
18	I enjoy reflecting on possibilities and philosophical ideas. (Green)	I believe in seizing the day, even if it means taking risks. (Orange)
19	I find contentment in understanding and accommodating others' emotions. (Blue)	I take pride in ensuring order and method in undertakings. (Gold)
20	I prioritize open and heartfelt communication. (Blue)	I appreciate reliability and dependable structures. (Gold)

21	I am energized by improvisation and shifting scenarios. (Orange)	I am content when environments are stable and predictable. (Gold)
22	I derive comfort from maintaining and respecting established systems. (Gold)	I believe in continuous learning and exploring innovative ideas. (Green)
23	I enjoy adapting to new, exhilarating situations on a whim. (Orange)	I appreciate methodical thinking and thorough problem solving. (Green)
24	I believe effective functioning arises from following established protocols. (Gold)	I think maintaining emotional harmony is a cornerstone for collective well-being. (Blue)

Excellent job in completing the assessment! Gaining a deeper understanding of yourself is a significant step towards personal growth. As you navigate through life's adventures, remember to celebrate your individuality and continue exploring the depths of your personality. The journey of self-discovery is always evolving—enjoy every moment!

Scoring

Count the Blue Answers. Begin by reviewing the answers and count every instance where the color Blue was selected. Write down the total number in the Blue box below.

Repeat for Each Color. Use the same process to tally the selections for Gold, Green, and Orange. Make sure to keep track of each color's total separately to avoid any confusion.

Identifying the Dominant Color. Identify which color has the highest total number—that color is most representative of your child's personality according to the quiz.

BLUE	GOLD	GREEN	ORANGE

The Blue Personality

- In my relationships, I ardently seek profound emotional connections, intertwined with shared values, and ardently believe in the idea of a soul-stirring, kindred spirit kind of love.

- Authenticity in every single one of my interactions stands non-negotiable; I fervently uphold and treasure genuine connections and deeply meaningful conversations above anything superficial.

- Empathy, to me, is more than an attribute; it's my distinctive superpower, always fervently aiming to understand and be an unwavering emotional pillar for others.

- My aspirations and dreams frequently reach beyond the immediate confines, embracing vast horizons of future potentials and endless possibilities.

- The profound depth of my feelings and emotions often propels me into the evocative realms of creativity, crafting artistic expressions that beautifully mirror the nuances of my inner world.

- I don't just like harmony; I deeply cherish it and consistently strive to nurture and foster peaceful, constructive environments in every setting I find myself in.

- The term "visionary" could easily be my middle name, as I often find myself lost in contemplation, pondering over future scenarios, potentials, and the myriad possibilities that lie ahead.

- When I delve into decision-making, my deeply embedded moral compass and steadfast values aren't just guiding lights; they act as unwavering, non-negotiable rules that I adhere to.

- My friendships extend beyond casual connections; they blossom into heartfelt, lasting bonds, meticulously nurtured with genuine care, deep understanding, and mutual respect.
- Coming of age, for me, isn't just a phase; it's a profound spiritual and emotional journey, intrinsically tied to the paths of self-discovery and personal growth.
- The blatant injustices and inequities of the world don't merely upset me; they fervently call me into action, compelling me towards causes that passionately seek to rectify these wrongs.
- In my romantic pursuits, I often find myself on a quest for a soulmate, yearning for someone capable of traversing the profound depths of emotions, feelings, and thoughts right alongside me.
- My ambitions are not confined to mere career goals; they're intricately intertwined with my personal growth journey and the potential positive impacts I can imprint upon the world.
- The essence of understanding and the quest to be profoundly understood underpin almost all my interactions, shaping the foundation of my relationships.
- I have an insatiable craving for deeply meaningful conversations, where words transcend their auditory essence and morph into a symphony of shared feelings and insightful revelations.
- My learning isn't restricted to structured academic pursuits but expansively spans the realms of understanding intricate human emotions, behaviors, and the delicate web of human connections.

- Compassion, for me, isn't merely a trait; it's a profound lens through which I perceive, understand, and interact with the multifaceted world around me.
- My deeply intuitive nature frequently guides my steps, allowing me to sense hidden patterns and unseen possibilities in the intricate tapestry of life's myriad interactions.
- An unwavering respect for all beings, regardless of any distinctions, forms a cornerstone of my beliefs, ensuring every action and word I utter mirrors this ethos consistently.
- When I step into a role of leadership, my approach is finely interwoven with deep empathy, seeking to inspire and galvanize others through mutual understanding and a shared, collective vision.
- My adventures resonate as soulful quests, actively seeking experiences that harmoniously resonate with my very essence and closely-held ideals.
- Ethical considerations and reflections continuously frame and shape my actions, ensuring they always remain in alignment with my deeply cherished beliefs and core moral values.
- Emotional intelligence emerges as more than a skill; for me, it's an invaluable navigation compass, aiding my journey through the world in a manner that's both meaningful and empathetic.
- I frequently find solace and comfort in diverse artistic expressions, whether it's art, soul-stirring music, or evocative writing, discovering reflections of my inner universe echoed within them.
- The unwavering pursuit of both personal and collective betterment forms a consistent part of my journey, as I ardently believe in the transformative potential of evolution and positive change

The Gold Personality

- I live in a world that thrives on structured routines, where the principles of reliability and consistency are the pillars that support my everyday life.
- I don't just perform my responsibilities; I take them seriously, consistently meeting every obligation with dedication and attention to detail.
- In relationships, I seek stability and commitment, valuing shared traditions and deeply-rooted moral values.
- Order in my life isn't just a preference; it's a fundamental need that underpins my daily routines and plans.
- Coming of age means forming a distinct identity aligned with my values and societal expectations.
- My distinct leadership style is firmly rooted in organization and structured approaches, ensuring every component and member operates cohesively for smooth, efficient functioning.
- Loyalty, to me, isn't just a simple virtue; it stands as a defining principle that shapes the contours of my friendships, bonds, and romantic relationships, ensuring lasting connections.
- I not only respect but ardently uphold and cherish traditions, viewing them as vital threads intricately weaving through the rich fabric of our shared experiences, memories, and collective histories.
- When it comes to career aspirations, mine are solidly and pragmatically anchored, always keeping in mind the notions of stability, long-term security, and my potential contribution to society.

- Being exceptionally meticulous and remarkably detail-oriented, I take pride in ensuring that every single task, whether big or minuscule, is executed with precision, accuracy, and thoroughness.
- For me, a strong sense of community and belonging is paramount; it's where I consistently find both a meaningful role to play and a robust network of unwavering support and solidarity.
- I'm a staunch believer in adopting a systematic and methodical approach to problems and challenges, ensuring each progressive step is logically thought out and sequentially planned.
- In my dating life, I always adopt a careful pace, taking things methodically and intentionally, ensuring at every step that both my partner and I share mutual understanding and are in complete alignment.
- Whenever conflicts or disagreements arise, I instinctively turn to time-tested protocols and accepted norms, leveraging them as guides to navigate through any turbulent waters.
- I hold family ties in the highest regard and visualize myself perpetuating, nurturing, and strengthening these sacred bonds throughout every stage of my life.
- My unwavering moral compass is not based on fleeting sentiments but is firmly aligned with established societal norms, ensuring that my actions and decisions consistently echo collective ethical beliefs and values.
- I don't just aim to complete tasks; I derive immense satisfaction and pride from a job meticulously well done, a reflection of my dedication to quality and my undying commitment to excellence.

- An intrinsic respect for authority and its pivotal role is integral to my worldview, acknowledging and appreciating the structure, order, and stability it consistently provides to the larger society.
- Planning for the future in my life isn't merely an occasional option; it's a continuous, unending process, a strategic effort ensuring that my path remains always clear, defined, and goal-oriented.
- In friendships and group dynamics, I often find myself as the anchoring individual who ensures that plans are systematically organized, executed, and that every participant is in sync and on the same page.
- I perceive social structures not just as constructs but as absolutely necessary frameworks, upholding a tried and tested system that has been refined and polished through the annals of time.
- My intrinsic sense of duty consistently transcends personal wants or desires, always prioritizing the collective needs, responsibilities, and the greater good of the organization.
- My decision-making process is comprehensive and involves a analysis of how potential choices and actions align with established norms and the expected, beneficial outcomes.
- In times of inevitable change, I approach alterations with caution and introspection, evaluating each modification to ensure they resonate harmoniously with my cherished values and holistic understanding.
- Whenever I'm a part of a team, my role often revolves around ensuring tasks are clearly outlined, efficiently delegated, and adhered to in a disciplined manner.

The Green Personality

- My mind is perpetually active and abuzz with innovative ideas, diving into the exploration of new concepts and eagerly probing into the depths of previously uncharted intellectual territories.
- Competence and a deep-seated intelligence are not just traits but my distinct calling cards, profoundly shaping the manner in which I navigate my personal relationships and professional pursuits.
- When it comes to matters of the heart, I earnestly seek a profound mental connection, yearning for intellectually stimulating conversations and a mutual passion for shared curiosities.
- The importance of autonomy cannot be overstated; I crave the unrestricted freedom to explore, innovate, and dive profoundly deep into the intricate web of my cascading thoughts and ideas.
- Coming of age, for me, signifies more than just growth; it means embracing my intellectual prowess and strategically utilizing it to carve a unique path forward in life.
- My interpersonal relationships, inclusive of dating, often center around the mutual exploration of complex ideas, engaging in in-depth thoughtful dialogue, and intellectual synergy.
- Even when navigating the murky waters of emotions, I inherently seek a semblance of rationality, striving to dissect and make sense of feelings through structured logic and comprehensive understanding.
- When I step into a leadership role, my approach is distinctively strategic and forward-thinking, ensuring that each decision is carefully calculated, and each potential risk is thoroughly measured and analyzed.

- I often find solace and inspiration in the abstract realms of thought, delving into theoretical concepts and allowing my imagination to envisage possibilities that stretch beyond the confines of the present.
- While I'm a dreamer, practicality is meticulously woven through my aspirations, ensuring that the goals I set for myself are both lofty in vision and realistically achievable.
- The concept of independence for me is holistic; it doesn't only pertain to my actions but extends to safeguarding my thoughts, ensuring they remain free, unbridled, and authentically mine.
- In all my communications, I place an unwavering value on precision, cherishing utmost clarity, and succinctness in articulating and conveying my intricate thoughts and ideas.
- While I'm predominantly rational in my approach, my passions and enthusiasms run profoundly deep, especially when the subject revolves around the boundless pursuits of knowledge, learning, and comprehensive understanding.
- With an analytical and critical mindset, I approach problems, dissecting multifaceted issues to comprehend their core essence and devise innovative, effective solutions.
- In the intricate tapestry of my relationships, I meticulously weave threads grounded in mutual respect for personal autonomy, intellectual freedom, and shared exploration.
- The foundation of my friendships often rests upon shared intellectual interests, mutual appreciation for analytical discussions, and a collective love for thought-provoking debates.

- When I venture into the realm of dating, I predominantly seek out partners who intellectually challenge and stimulate me, and who resonate with my boundless explorative curiosity.
- My moral stances and ethical considerations undergo rigorous scrutiny, examined and assessed through a lens of logical consistency, rationality, and broad universal applicability.
- Career avenues that consistently stimulate my intellect, challenge my analytical and problem-solving capabilities, and offer a platform for innovation hold the most allure for me.
- I maintain an openness to entertaining new ideas and unconventional paths, provided they're logically sound, coherently structured, and intellectually stimulating.
- To me, a day that goes by without acquiring new knowledge, without exploring a novel idea or concept, feels like an opportunity missed, a day not fully realized.
- Strategy isn't just a tool; I deeply relish in it, drawing immense intellectual stimulation and satisfaction from intricate planning, foresight, and envisioning future scenarios.
- My lofty aspirations are not merely fleeting dreams; they're meticulously crafted visions of the future that I thoroughly dissect, analyze, and strategize for.
- Even in moments of emotional uncertainty or turbidity, I find a way to ground and anchor myself through deep introspection, structured analysis, and rational comprehension.
- My personal growth is tied to intellectual expansion, guiding my path with knowledge and understanding.

The Orange Personality

- Life for me is a thrilling adventure, and I'm always on the lookout, ready to dive into the next exhilarating opportunity that presents itself.
- Together with my friends, we embrace the spontaneity of life, fully enjoying each spontaneous moment without the burden of worrying about the distant future.
- Coming of age for me means eagerly embracing my growing independence and taking the plunge into the vast array of enriching experiences life generously presents.
- When it comes to the realm of dating, I dive in with a zest for fun and thrill, ensuring every date is packed with laughter, joy, and unforgettable moments.
- Thanks to my natural charm and infectious enthusiasm, I often find people naturally gravitating towards me, creating a lively social circle that's always alive with energy and excitement.
- Being flexible is crucial for me; I pride myself on my ability to smoothly go with the flow, embracing the winds of change and adapting to fresh scenarios without hesitation.
- While I deeply value and cherish my close relationships, ensuring I have personal freedom to explore and dive into various experiences remains at the forefront for me.
- In academic or professional settings, I particularly shine when given practical, hands-on tasks, where I can directly employ my sharp problem-solving abilities in a creative manner.

- My energy seems endless, perpetually fueled and always on standby, ready to kickstart a new expedition or adapt to an unforeseen change in course.
- Often, I find myself as the main catalyst for lively social activities, seamlessly bringing diverse groups of people together for fun-filled, spirited, and spontaneous events.
- Charting my own path, I rely heavily on my sharp intuition and instinctual gut feelings, having full faith in my capacity to adeptly adapt and react to any curveball life throws.
- Living in the moment is my mantra; not held back by any past regrets or undue worry about the unforeseen future, I am completely engrossed in the vibrant present.
- My charisma serves a dual purpose; while being a magnetic social trait, it also aids me in skillfully navigating a myriad of challenges and seizing opportunities with unparalleled flair.
- I possess a keen interest in experimenting with various facets of my identity, ranging from exploring eclectic hobbies, diverse fashion styles, to mingling in a variety of social circles.
- When it comes to romantic relationships, I'm on the lookout for a partner equally adventurous, someone who's ready to share in the spontaneous escapades and thrilling moments that await.
- My decisive nature is heavily influenced by the immediate context, evaluating situations promptly and taking actions based on the most enticing opportunities the present offers.

- My preferred learning style is experiential; I thrive when I can engage directly, immersing myself in activities that offer a hands-on approach to understanding and applying new concepts.
- Every relationship I forge is like an exciting new journey, offering a fresh opportunity to explore shared interests in an enthusiastic, candid manner.
- I eagerly accept challenges head-on, employing my knack for improvisation to devise spontaneous solutions, turning obstacles into opportunities.
- My loyalty runs deep; standing steadfastly by my friends' sides, I am always primed for action, ready to extend my support whenever they find themselves in a bind.
- While there's an aspect of my life where I appreciate the comfort of stability, my soul predominantly hungers for diversity, ensuring each passing day offers unique experiences and exploration avenues.
- Risks don't deter me; instead, I embrace them, often venturing boldly into uncharted territories if they hint at an exhilarating adventure or a riveting new experience.
- In my professional journey and personal pursuits, I'm drawn to roles that provide an opportunity to harness my tactical acumen, coupled with a hands-on approach to problem-solving.
- More often than not, my zestful spirit uplifts those around me, serving as a motivating force that urges them to step beyond their boundaries and embrace the world of unknowns.
- As I continue my journey forward, my boundless energy, zest for adventure, and innate adaptability serve as my guiding light, leading me through the exhilarating journey that is life.

Chapter 16

What's Next?

As this book concludes, it paves the way for *Insightful Parenting 2*, its sequel that dives deeper into real-life applications of parenting strategies. It offers practical approaches for various scenarios, ensuring your parenting evolves with your child's unique temperament. The journey continues with enriched understanding and actionable insights for everyday parenting challenges.

Reflecting on Our Parenting Journey

As we conclude our journey through this book, let's take a moment to reflect on the valuable insights and newfound understanding we've gained. This book has not just been a source of information; it has been a transformative guide in how we approach parenting. Here's a recap of the essential lessons and the benefits that you, as a reader, now possess from this enlightening experience.

The Pillar of Adaptive Parenting

Central to the book's teachings is the concept of adaptive parenting. This approach, emphasizing flexibility and responsiveness, has shown us that the traditional one-size-fits-all method falls short in addressing the unique needs of each child. As a result of this understanding, you're now equipped to tailor your parenting style to harmonize with both your child's temperament and your personal characteristics.

Navigating Through Parenting Styles

The exploration of the four parenting styles—Blue, Gold, Green, and Orange—has been an eye-opener. This journey has helped you identify and appreciate the distinct qualities of each style:

- Blue Parents shine with empathy and nurturing, creating emotionally safe spaces.
- Gold Parents provide stability and structure, valuing traditions and clear rules.
- Green Parents foster intellectual growth and curiosity, encouraging logical thinking.
- Orange Parents bring energy and spontaneity, focusing on adventure and enjoyment.

Understanding these styles has empowered you to recognize your natural parenting inclinations and how they align or differ from your child's temperament.

Insights into Parent-Child Dynamics

One of the most impactful aspects of the book is its exploration of the interaction between various parenting styles and children's temperaments. You've gained insights into potential challenges and learned the importance of adapting your approach to foster harmonious relationships. This knowledge has equipped you to better understand and respond to your child's unique needs and behaviors.

The Multifaceted Nature of Parenting

The book acknowledges the complexities and diverse scenarios of modern parenting, including single parenting and co-parenting dynamics. You've learned the importance of empathy, respect, and balance in nurturing children with varied temperaments, a lesson that enriches your parenting toolkit.

Realizing the Benefits of Adaptive Parenting

Through adaptive parenting, you've learned the art of building resilient relationships and fostering an environment of empathy and understanding. This approach has not only enriched the emotional climate of your household but also promoted mutual growth and understanding among family members.

Engagement and Reflection for Personal Growth

Finally, the book has been more than a guide; it's been a companion on your personal growth journey. The interactive reflections and insights have encouraged you to deeply understand your parenting style and to adapt and evolve in response to your children's needs.

As you reflect on these lessons, remember that the journey of parenting is ongoing. The insights and strategies you've gained from this book are tools that will continue to guide and inspire you as you navigate the ever-evolving landscape of raising children.

Unlocking New Dimensions

Having journeyed through the insightful and transformative world of *Insightful Parenting 1*, you might be wondering, "What's next?" How can you further refine your parenting approach to align even more closely with your child's unique temperament? The answer lies in the pages of *Insightful Parenting 2*. Here's why delving into this sequel is not just a good idea but an essential step in your parenting journey.

1. Deep Dive into Individual Temperaments

While this book laid a solid foundation in temperament-based parenting, *Insightful Parenting 2* takes you deeper. Imagine a tool that doesn't just identify your child's temperament but also gives you a detailed roadmap for nurturing it. This second book does exactly that. It provides specific strategies and insights tailored to each temperament, empowering you to connect with your child on a level you never thought possible. You've learned the basics; now it's time to master the art.

2. Comprehensive Coverage

Parenting, in its essence, is a multifaceted journey. *Insightful Parenting 2* recognizes this by covering a broader range of topics, from understanding stressors unique to each temperament to navigating the challenges of technology in parenting. This holistic approach ensures that no stone is left unturned, equipping you to handle the diverse aspects of your child's personality with confidence and grace.

3. Practical Applications

Theory is essential, but practical application is key. Every chapter in this book is packed with actionable advice and strategies. Whether it's dealing with a stubborn toddler, a rebellious teenager, or anything in between, you'll find hands-on tips and techniques that you can implement immediately. This book isn't just a read; it's a hands-on guide to better parenting.

4. Tailored Approaches

Every child is unique, and so are the challenges they present. *Insightful Parenting 2* offers tailored advice for an array of situations, helping you adapt your parenting style to suit your child's individual needs and temperament. This tailored approach means you're always prepared, whether it's a regular day at the park or navigating the more challenging waters of adolescence.

5. Fostering Deeper Connections

The heart of effective parenting lies in the connection you share with your child. This book helps deepen that connection by providing insights into how to communicate more effectively, understand their deeper emotional needs, and foster stronger bonds. It's about building a relationship that transcends the typical parent-child dynamic, creating a lifelong bond based on mutual respect and understanding.

6. Balanced Parenting Strategies

Insightful Parenting 2 presents a balanced view of critical aspects of parenting, such as discipline, motivation, and emotional support. These balanced strategies are vital for nurturing well-rounded, confident, and happy individuals. The book teaches you how to strike the perfect balance between guidance and freedom, ensuring your child's holistic development.

7. Inclusivity in Parenting

In today's diverse world, inclusivity in parenting is more important than ever. This book addresses the needs of children with various temperaments in different areas of life, from academic to leisure, ensuring that your parenting approach is as diverse and inclusive as the world we live in.

Insightful Parenting 2 is not just a sequel—it's a necessary extension of your parenting journey. It builds on the foundations laid form this book, taking your understanding to new heights and equipping you with the tools and strategies you need for the ever-evolving adventure of parenting. Would you like more details on exactly what those strategies are? Keep reading.

What's Inside Each Chapter?

Family Activities. This chapter guides you in planning family activities that cater to each child's unique temperament, creating a harmonious and inclusive family environment. It provides ideas for activities that resonate with different temperaments, ensuring every family member feels engaged and valued. The goal is to foster stronger bonds and create memorable experiences that reflect the diverse interests within the family.

Stressors. Explores how various temperaments perceive and react to stress, providing insights into identifying and managing these stressors in children and teenagers. The chapter offers strategies for parents to support their children in developing resilience and understanding. It emphasizes the importance of a nuanced approach to stress, recognizing that what may be stressful for one temperament may not be for another.

Effective Discipline. Advocates for a nuanced approach to discipline, tailored to the unique temperament of each child. It emphasizes the importance of understanding a child's intrinsic motivations and behaviors to guide them effectively. This chapter provides practical strategies for teaching and guiding children, moving away from punitive measures to more constructive and empathetic methods.

Communication Style. Delves into the different communication styles of children and teenagers, shaped by their temperament. It underscores the significance of understanding these styles for more effective and empathetic parenting. This chapter offers insights into enhancing communication, fostering deeper connections, and addressing the unique ways children express their thoughts and feelings.

Learning Preferences. Addresses how various temperaments influence children's approach to learning and educational engagement. It provides strategies for adapting teaching methods and learning environments to suit different learning styles. The focus is on optimizing educational experiences by aligning them with the child's natural inclinations and preferences.

Conflict Resolution. Focuses on conflict resolution strategies that consider the diverse temperaments of children. This chapter helps parents navigate disagreements and conflicts by understanding the underlying temperamental traits that drive children's reactions. It offers practical tips for mediating conflicts in a way that respects and acknowledges each child's perspective.

Social Interaction. Analyzes the impact of temperament on children's social interactions and relationships. It explores how different temperaments navigate social situations, friendships, and group dynamics. The chapter provides insights into guiding children in developing healthy social skills that align with their natural tendencies.

Emotional Expression. Examines the varied ways in which children with different temperaments express their emotions. It offers guidance on recognizing and responding to these expressions in a supportive and understanding manner. The chapter aims to help parents foster emotional intelligence and expression in their children.

Motivation and Goal Setting. Discusses strategies for motivating children and setting goals that resonate with their temperament. It emphasizes the importance of aligning expectations and ambitions with the child's natural inclinations and strengths. This chapter provides insights into nurturing a child's intrinsic motivation and helping them set and achieve realistic and fulfilling goals.

Creativity and Problem Solving. Offers insights into nurturing the creative and problem-solving abilities of children, considering their temperamental traits. It explores how different temperaments approach creativity and problem-solving, providing strategies for encouraging these skills in a supportive and conducive environment. The chapter aims to foster innovation and critical thinking in children.

Leisure Activities and Hobbies. Suggests a variety of leisure activities and hobbies tailored to different temperament styles, encouraging parents to support their children's interests. The chapter emphasizes the importance of recognizing and nurturing individual passions and hobbies for overall well-being and development. It provides ideas for activities that cater to each temperament, ensuring children engage in fulfilling and enjoyable pastimes.

Response to Authority. Looks at how children with different temperaments respond to authority figures and structured environments, offering insights for parents and educators. This chapter explores the dynamics of authority and compliance in relation to temperament, providing strategies for effective communication and guidance. It emphasizes the importance of understanding and respecting each child's natural response to authority.

Stress Management and Coping Strategies. Provides effective techniques for managing stress, tailored to suit different temperaments. This chapter helps parents identify signs of stress in their children and offers tools for helping them cope in healthy and constructive ways. It emphasizes the importance of nurturing resilience and emotional intelligence.

Organizational Skills. Discusses strategies for developing organizational skills in children, taking into account their temperament. The chapter provides practical tips for helping children manage their time, tasks, and responsibilities in a way that aligns with their natural tendencies. It aims to foster a sense of responsibility and self-management in a supportive and understanding environment.

Empathy and Compassion. Focuses on fostering empathy and compassion in children, considering their temperamental differences. This chapter emphasizes the importance of nurturing emotional intelligence and understanding in children, teaching them to empathize with and understand others. It provides strategies for parents to model and encourage these values in everyday interactions.

Risk-Taking and Adventure Seeking. Explores how to manage and guide children's natural tendencies towards risk-taking and adventure, based on their temperament. The chapter offers insights into balancing the need for safety with the desire for exploration and excitement. It provides strategies for encouraging healthy risk-taking and adventure-seeking behaviors.

Responsibility and Reliability. Addresses the teaching of responsibility and reliability in children, influenced by their temperament. This chapter provides strategies for instilling a sense of duty and dependability in children, tailored to their natural inclinations. It emphasizes the importance of nurturing these traits for long-term personal development and success.

Adaptability and Change. Focuses on helping children develop adaptability and resilience to change, considering their temperament. The chapter offers insights into how different temperaments cope with change and provides strategies for supporting children through transitions and new experiences. It emphasizes the importance of fostering flexibility and open-mindedness.

Academic Interests. Looks at how a child's temperament affects their academic interests and approaches to learning. This chapter provides strategies for nurturing a child's natural curiosity and strengths in academic settings. It emphasizes the importance of aligning educational experiences with a child's inherent interests and abilities.

Leadership Style. Analyzes the different leadership styles that emerge from various temperaments, providing insights for parents and educators. This chapter explores how to nurture leadership qualities in children, considering their natural tendencies and strengths. It offers strategies for encouraging responsible and effective leadership skills.

Sense of Humor. Explores how a child's temperament influences their sense of humor, providing insights into understanding and nurturing this aspect of their personality. The chapter discusses the importance of humor in social and emotional development. It offers tips for parents to engage with and support their child's unique sense of humor.

Decision-Making Process. Discusses the decision-making styles of different temperaments, offering insights into how to support children in developing effective decision-making skills. The chapter provides strategies for encouraging independent thought and responsible decision-making. It emphasizes the importance of understanding a child's natural approach to making choices.

Independence vs. Dependence. Examines the spectrum of independence and dependence across temperaments, providing insights into nurturing a balanced approach. The chapter discusses how to encourage autonomy in children while providing the necessary support and guidance. It emphasizes the importance of respecting a child's natural inclinations towards independence or reliance.

Self-Esteem and Self-Image. Focuses on how temperament affects a child's self-esteem and self-image, offering strategies for nurturing positive self-perception. The chapter discusses the role of temperament in shaping a child's view of themselves and their abilities. It provides tips for reinforcing positive self-esteem and addressing insecurities.

Attention and Focus. Addresses strategies for improving attention and focus in children, considering their temperament. The chapter provides insights into how different temperaments affect a child's ability to concentrate and stay on task. It offers practical tips for helping children develop better focus and attention skills.

Relationship with Technology. Explores the relationship between children's technology use and their temperament, offering insights into managing screen time and digital interactions. The chapter discusses how temperament influences a child's engagement with technology and provides strategies for healthy technology use.

Athleticism and Physical Activity. Looks at how temperament influences a child's interest and engagement in physical activities and sports. The chapter offers insights into nurturing a child's natural athletic tendencies and finding physical activities that align with their temperament. It emphasizes the importance of physical activity for overall health and well-being.

Artistic Expression. Examines how different temperaments influence a child's artistic expressions and interests. The chapter provides strategies for nurturing a child's artistic abilities and creativity. It emphasizes the importance of art in emotional and cognitive development.

Spirituality and Religion. This chapter delves into how a child's temperament influences their approach to spirituality and religion. It discusses the varying ways children with different temperaments engage with spiritual practices and religious teachings. The aim is to guide parents in nurturing their child's spiritual growth in a way that resonates with their innate personality.

Future Orientation and Aspirations. This section focuses on the impact of temperament on children's outlook towards their future and their aspirations. It explores how different personality types envision their future, set goals, and work towards them, offering insights for parents to support their child's dreams and ambitions effectively. The chapter emphasizes the importance of aligning parental guidance with the child's natural tendencies and aspirations.

Embracing the Journey of Insightful Parenting

As we draw the curtain on this enlightening journey with *Insightful Parenting 1*, we find ourselves standing at the threshold of a new understanding, equipped with tools not just to parent but to nurture. This book has been more than a guide; it has been a companion, illuminating the path to a deeper connection with our children. It's a journey that's taught us the beauty of seeing the world through our children's eyes, appreciating their unique temperaments, and adapting our parenting to honor their individuality.

Parenting, we've learned, isn't just about guiding our children; it's about growing with them. Each chapter has offered us a mirror to reflect on our own attitudes and behaviors, challenging us to evolve and embrace the multifaceted roles we play. From the empathetic nurturer to the adventurous guide, we've seen aspects of ourselves in every hue of parenting. This book has shown us that our children are not just ours to teach, but they are also our teachers, constantly inviting us to view life in vibrant colors we never knew existed.

As you move forward, remember that the journey of parenting is perpetual, filled with both challenges and triumphs. The lessons learned from *Insightful Parenting 1* are your companions in this continuous voyage. May you find joy in every moment of discovery, strength in every challenge, and fulfillment in witnessing the beautiful unfolding of your child's unique journey. Here's to parenting not just with wisdom but with insight, empathy, and an ever-adaptive heart.

Made in the USA
Columbia, SC
07 December 2023